IMAGES
of America

WESTMINSTER

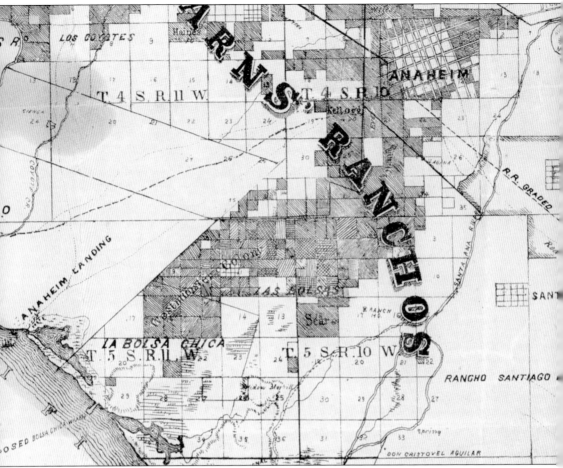

This map shows the location of Westminster Colony (below and left of center in the photograph), then five years old, in 1876. The shaded areas are property sold by the Stearns Ranchos, and the small white area in the center of the colony was the village center near Westminster Boulevard and Olive Street. Anaheim Landing (at the left margin), near today's Seal Beach, was an important if unreliable port for goods for the few towns and settlements that existed in what is now Orange County. At this time, Anaheim was well established, and Westminster's population of about 500 people was comparable to Santa Ana's. (Courtesy Westminster Historical Museum.)

ON THE COVER: In 1918, Westminster's commercial center was still near Almond Street (now Westminster Boulevard) and Olive Street. This was the center of the original colony village and would remain the town's center of gravity until New Westminster started developing at Beach Boulevard and Westminster Boulevard around 1930. The city entered the suburban era with no discernible downtown. Despite the development of Little Saigon, it lacks one to this day. On the north side of the street (right), the small building with the peaked roof is now the site of the Mendez Tribute Monument Park. (Courtesy Westminster Historical Society.)

IMAGES
of America

WESTMINSTER

Nick Popadiuk

ARCADIA
PUBLISHING

Published by Arcadia Publishing
Charleston, South Carolina

Printed in the United States of America

Library of Congress Control Number: 2022951999

For all general information, please contact Arcadia Publishing:
Telephone 843-853-2070
Fax 843-853-0044
E-mail sales@arcadiapublishing.com
For customer service and orders:
Toll-Free 1-888-313-2665

Visit us on the Internet at www.arcadiapublishing.com

This book is for Colin, Elisa, and Gordon
and for Janice

CONTENTS

ACKNOWLEDGMENTS

This book would not have been possible without the cooperation and help of the Westminster Historical Society. Unless otherwise noted, all images appear courtesy of the Westminster Historical Museum. Curator Steve Iverson's knowledge, expertise, and editorial skills were crucial to its realization. Diane Tollefson's friendship, experience, and perspective were also a reliable resource. Joy Neugebauer provided encouragement during early stages of my research.

Chris Jepsen at the Orange County Archives was a supporter of my early efforts. It may have been his idea that I write this book; I am still not sure. Thanks to his assistant Steve Oftelie at the archives, too.

A list of people, by no means exhaustive, who helped along the way includes Tim Castroreale, Bob Ash, Bob Black, Beverly Fournier, Al Vela, Jim Tortolano, and a host of others.

Thanks is given to Sylvia Mendez and Janice Munemitsu for their permission to use photographs. And thanks especially to numerous librarians and archivists at sources mentioned in credit lines.

And thanks, as always, to Dr. Lawrence Siordia for his tea and sympathy.

INTRODUCTION

The earliest inhabitants of the Westminster area were Gabrielino (also known as Tongva) Native Americans. In 1938, under the Works Progress Administration, the Orange County Anthropological Project made preliminary archaeological survey notes for several Native American sites located in Westminster. They were situated mainly in the area of Bolsa Avenue and stretched from Santa Ana almost to Anaheim Landing at what is now the Seal Beach Weapons Station. Concentrations of artifacts and other evidence showed larger sites in Midway City and near the northeast corner of Beach and Westminster Boulevards. Many of the sites were small, seasonal hunting camps. A major religious center for Native Americans in the Los Angeles basin was a few miles away in the vicinity of the California State University, Long Beach campus.

Spanish colonization resulted in a mass displacement and decimation of the indigenous population. The Native Americans had all but disappeared from the area by the time Nieto's rancho was partitioned into six sections in 1834. Rancho Las Bolsas consisted of future Garden Grove, Huntington Beach, Westminster, and parts of other cities. It was granted to Manuel Nieto's widowed daughter-in-law Catarina Ruiz de Nieto. One of the conditions of rancho ownership was the construction of a ranch house. The ranch house for Las Bolsas was in present-day Little Saigon, not far from the intersection of Bolsa and Magnolia Avenues.

During the 1850s, Abel Stearns was the wealthiest man in Los Angeles County. He was in the state assembly, and he was on the county board of supervisors. In 1852, he bought Rancho Las Bolsas at an auction, and in the following years, he acquired other ranchos. He had close to 200,000 acres of cattle ranches when the drought and resultant famine of 1863–1864 killed his herds and sent him into deep debt. He was rescued from bankruptcy by a group of investors in San Francisco who assigned Stearns's old friend and business associate Alfred Robinson as trustee. In 1868, the Stearns Ranchos, as the property in what would become Orange County was called, were subdivided into 40-acre-minimum lots and sold by Robinson at $10–$20 an acre. The terms attracted a wave of pioneers and settlers into the area.

Lemuel Webber, Westminster's founder, was born in Salem County, New Jersey, in 1832. He moved to Ohio and became a Presbyterian minister when he was almost 28 years old. Two years later, he married Martha Elizabeth Jacquette. A short while after successfully leading a congregation in Indiana, he and his wife moved west, where earlier settlers had little spiritual guidance. While crossing the Isthmus of Panama on their way to San Francisco, the couple probably contracted the disease that would lead to their deaths.

The Webbers' newborn child passed away in Nevada, while Martha became increasingly sick. After Webber took charge of a new church in Santa Clara, his wife died in 1865. During this period, he formulated the idea of a colony of like-minded Christians for whom honesty, education, and cooperation were paramount. He traveled California looking at likely spots in which to establish his new colony.

Returning to New Jersey, Webber married his wife's sister Maria Jacquette in 1868, and a year later, he visited Anaheim for the first time. Soon he was invited to become pastor of the Anaheim

Presbyterian Church. He and Maria had a newborn son in Anaheim the following year. In October 1870, Webber selected a location between Anaheim and Anaheim Landing, near present-day Seal Beach, taking an option on 6,500 acres of land. It was here that Webber watched his vision of an agriculturally based community that shared their religious faith take form in Westminster Colony.

One

THE COLONY PERIOD
1870–1879

Westminster Colony was founded by Presbyterian minister Rev. Lemuel P. Webber in 1870.

He stated his "cherished purpose" for it in his "Prospectus of Westminster Colony, Los Angeles, Cal.": The colony would be a place where "persons of like views, in regard to the value of morals, founded upon the Bible" could cooperate and form an agriculture-based, "well-regulated society, and enjoy the most permanent prosperity." Webber located the colony about midway between Anaheim and Anaheim Landing, now at the US naval station at Seal Beach. He obtained control of 6,500 acres of property owned by the Stearns Ranchos from the Los Angeles and San Bernardino Land Company in October 1870 and served as an agent for them. Farms were sold at current market value ($13 an acre) in 40-, 80-, and 160-acre lots surrounding a town center of smaller lots located along a main road running east and west. Webber was clear that a settler's adherence to Christian tenets was essential. While not strictly a temperance town, members had to "solemnly pledge not to manufacture, buy or sell intoxicating beverages or liquor."

Webber's promotion of the colony, along with word of mouth, inspired a slow and steady stream of new settlers. Most of the pioneers were Presbyterians or Methodists who originated from the Midwest and Northeast. After setbacks during the colony's initial year, the first artesian well was bored in May 1871, and by 1879, there were 250 of them. The presence of a reliable source of water provided sustainability and was a great boon to farmers who already had potentially very productive soil. But Anaheim Landing would prove to be an unreliable resource for transportation of goods, an issue that would persist for decades after.

Westminster Colony survived for four years after Reverend Webber's death in 1874. Webber's passing and other factors contributed to the colony's demise. When Robert Strong resigned as superintendent in 1879, the colony's population was around 660. It would remain close to that until just before the turn of the 20th century.

Rev. Lemuel Webber, founder and supervisor of Westminster Colony, was born in Salem County, New Jersey, in 1832. He married Martha Jaquette in 1862, and the next year, he began a church in Austin, Nevada. They lost their child shortly before Martha passed away in Santa Clara, where Webber had begun another church, in 1865. Webber married his wife's sister in 1868, and in 1870, they moved to Anaheim, where he was offered a pastorate of a new church. He divided his efforts between his pastorate of the church in Anaheim and his new colony until his death in 1874. (Courtesy of Malcolm Sharp.)

John Yuell Anderson and his wife, Virginia, were the first settlers in Westminster Colony. Also pictured are their children, Mary and Harry. Originally from Virginia, where John had fought for the South in the Civil War, they moved into the settlement's first home on what is now Monroe Street in November 1870. The first Presbyterian services in the colony were held by Reverend Webber in the Andersons' home in 1871. John built a sorghum mill that was one of the earliest commercial efforts in the colony. He later joined the locally burgeoning dairy industry. Virginia passed away in Westminster in 1889, and in his later years, John moved to Santa Ana. He died at his daughter's home in Los Angeles in 1920.

Henry Stephens was born in England in 1827 and immigrated to the United States in 1851. He married Olive Shaw from Pennsylvania in 1865. They moved from Stockton to settle with little initial capital in early Westminster Colony in 1871. They bought property on Newland Street, which would later become the site of Friendly Dairy. The home they built was considered one of the finest in the colony. He became a successful dairy farmer, merchant, and partner at the Westminster Cooperative Store. He and his wife were prosperous and active members of the Congregationalist church.

Westminster's first schoolhouse, located in Sigler Park, was built and opened in 1872 at a cost of $1,500. The first class had 13 students taught by Converse Howe, a recent arrival to the colony. About five percent of the soil in Westminster contained alkali, and it was present in the grounds surrounding the school. Complaints from barefooted students about burning feet prompted community members to clear up the area. By 1879, when Westminster School District was formed, there were already discussions about building a larger schoolhouse to accommodate the township's anticipated growth.

Annalist, surveyor and mapmaker, and local tax collector Walter "Frank" Poor was a bachelor when he took on some of the leadership roles of the new colony. He came from Oakland in late 1871 and bought 40 acres of land. He was an active member of the Grange and served as its secretary and treasurer. He was also a correspondent for the *Anaheim Gazette* during the colony's later period. He married fellow colonist Addie Leffler in 1879, and they had a daughter less than a year later. The family left Westminster in 1880 to reside in San Gabriel. In 1900, they moved to Highland Park, where he engaged in real estate.

Dr. James McCoy, Westminster's first physician, arrived at Westminster Colony from Illinois with his wife, Clementine, in 1873 at the request of Reverend Webber. He and Dr. James Gregory opened Westminster's second drugstore on Westminster Boulevard in 1877, a year after Dr. Alvin and Dr. Phillip Howe opened theirs. He would later maintain a home for invalids. He and Clementine later retired to Beaumont, California, where he passed away in 1894. McCoy's Pharmacy, today located at the Leaora Blakey Historical Park, is the oldest building still standing in Westminster.

Clementine Marquis McCoy was born in Illinois in 1837. She married James McCoy, 21 years her senior, in their home state of Illinois. Her father, Rev. John Marquis, was the first settler to purchase property on the 160 acres set aside as a townsite surrounding the Plaza (now called Sigler Park). Her brother Waldo married Ferdinand Kiefhaber's daughter Minnie, and her sister Dapsileia married schoolteacher and historian James Guinn. After the death of her husband, she moved to Nevada, where she died in 1916.

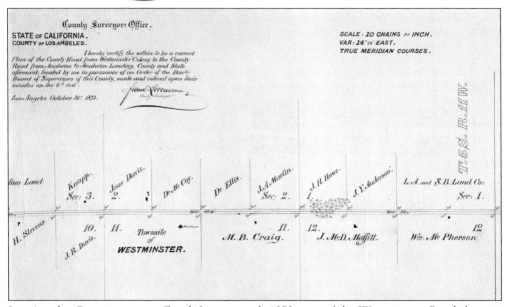

Los Angeles County surveyor Frank Lecouvreur's 1873 map of the Westminster Road shows it running east and west through the fledgling village center of Westminster Colony. There are several houses and the schoolhouse in the Plaza (now Sigler Park), where the map reads "Townsite of Westminster." On the southern portion of J.H. Howe's property on the northeast corner of Beach Boulevard and Westminster Boulevard can be seen one of the swampy areas that were widespread in the colony. Westminster Drainage District would not be formed until 1915. (Courtesy Huntington Library, San Marino, California.)

Judge Josia McCoy was an insurance agent and Westminster's first justice of the peace. Coming from Illinois, he settled in the colony shortly after the arrival of his brother James in 1873. He was politically active, attending county conventions as a delegate from Westminster's precinct. He served the Presbyterian church as an elder, Sunday school superintendent, and teacher until he passed away in 1908 at the age of 82.

Hattie McCoy Burlingame was the daughter of Judge Josia McCoy. She was a music teacher and composer. In 1902, at the age of 33, she married Anson Burlingame, a grocery store keeper from Healdsburg, California. They lived in Healdsburg for a few years before relocating to Westminster. They remodeled Hattie's uncle James's old drugstore and made it their home for a short period. They eventually moved to Long Beach, where Hattie passed away in 1917. Anson Burlingame died 22 years later and is buried in Healdsburg.

Walter Sherwood's father, James, was one of the earliest pioneers in the colony. He arrived in 1871 and married Mary McFadden at the home of the bride's family the following year. Theirs was the first marriage that took place in Westminster, performed by the colony founder, Reverend Webber. Walter was born in July 1873. His father was a trustee of the Presbyterian church and became superintendent when Rev. George Mack resigned.

Ferdinand Kiefhaber was a strict Presbyterian and the colony's first blacksmith. He and his brother learned the trade in Pennsylvania before moving to Illinois with his first wife, Margaret. After she died in 1871, he married Maria Bussard in 1873. At the request of Reverend Webber, he and his family relocated to the new colony in October 1874. Kiefhaber was a staunch temperance supporter who reportedly allowed a crop of grapes to rot rather than sell them to make wine. He was a successful farmer and rancher who passed away in Westminster in 1904.

Ferdinand Kiefhaber's second wife, Maria Bussard, was born in Pennsylvania in 1839. Her mother and father were from Pennsylvania and Maryland. Ferdinand had five children when she married him and moved to Westminster. They had two children together, Frederick and Warren, who were both born in the colony. Maria moved to Los Angeles shortly after her husband's death and died there in 1919.

Upon their arrival in 1874, the Kiefhabers built a home while staying with the McCoys and Andersons. Shortly afterward, Ferdinand built the village's first blacksmith shop and soon added a wagon shop. The improvements made on Kiefhaber's ranch, including planting several different trees, draining a pond, and grading the property, were much admired by colony residents. Shown in the photograph are the Kiefhaber couple and their two sons.

As Reverend Webber's health failed, Rev. Robert Strong's position in the community became centrally important. He took over as superintendent of the colony on Webber's death and would keep the position until 1878. He was a tireless promoter of the settlement, writing glowing reviews for several newspapers and acting as correspondent for the *Anaheim Gazette*. His nursery northeast of Goldenwest Street and Westminster Boulevard was Westminster's first industry and became a hub of agricultural innovation. Strong was one of the first farmers to use gypsum to combat the alkali in the local soil. He was an early planter and seller of eucalyptus trees as windbreaks in the area. He, Reverend Webber, and Rev. John Marquis began the first Presbyterian church in the settlement. He would later marry Marquis's daughter Arvilla in 1875. He moved in 1889 to Pasadena, where he retired.

Upon arriving in Westminster in 1875, Sylvester and Nettie (Pollock) Lyman bought 600 acres on Beach Boulevard between Trask Avenue and Westminster Boulevard. They developed this into one of the more successful farms in the settlement. He was a trustee in the local Grange and, with John Anderson and William McPherson, discovered a large deposit of gypsum in the Santa Ana Mountains. The Lymans started a mercantile business two years before Sylvester's death in 1889. Nettie Lyman remained in Westminster following her husband's passing. The farm continued to prosper, and in 1904, she became part owner of the Arrowhead Springs Hotel in Lake Arrowhead.

RESIDENCE & FARM OF S. LYMAN, WESTMINSTER, LOS ANGELES Co CAL.

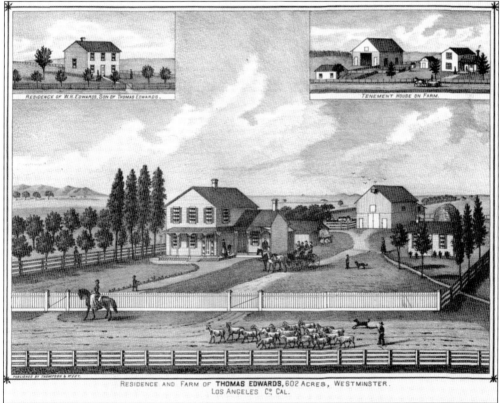

RESIDENCE OF W.H. EDWARDS, SON OF THOMAS EDWARDS.

TENEMENT HOUSE ON FARM.

RESIDENCE AND FARM OF THOMAS EDWARDS, 602 ACRES, WESTMINSTER. LOS ANGELES Co CAL.

Thomas Edwards was the first of the Edwards family to move to Westminster. He married Sarah Rogers in 1848, and they moved to northern California shortly after the Gold Rush. He worked in gold mines until they moved to the colony in 1872. They bought 600 acres, which they farmed. In 1874, he had the largest well in Westminster, drilled to a depth of 84 feet. In 1877, they started one of the early dairy ranches in the colony. He was a trustee of the Presbyterian church during this period. Thomas Edwards passed away in Los Angeles in 1906.

Samson and Diana Edwards were born in England and met and married in the United States in 1851. They arrived in Westminster Colony from Illinois in 1874, two years after their son John had settled there. The patriarch of the Edwards family found success raising dairy cattle and selling meat. By the time this photograph was taken commemorating their 50th anniversary, they had moved to Santa Ana. Samson was an early grower of eucalyptus trees in the area and reportedly brought the first automobile to Westminster. They died in Santa Ana in an accident with a Pacific Electric Red Car in 1912. (Courtesy First American Title Insurance Company.)

Letitia Penhall, the matriarch of Westminster's Penhall family, was born in 1837 in Wales, Great Britain. She and her husband, Uriah, a miner from Australia, met and married in England before joining the Gold Rush in California after 1849. In 1873, they bought 60 acres of land near Goldenwest Street and Bolsa Avenue next to the Edwards and Larter properties. The Penhalls were Methodists, and Uriah was a trustee when the Methodists built the first church in Westminster. He died in 1891, and Letitia passed away in 1915. They are both buried at Magnolia Memorial Park.

In 1907, the arrival of the Southern Pacific Railroad forced the removal of the Samson and Diane Edwards home at Hoover Street and Westminster Boulevard. The prosperous couple were living in Santa Ana by the time of their 50th wedding anniversary in 1901. In 1905, Edwards had liquidated his ranch and auctioned off farming implements and equipment.

John H. Edwards, son of Samson and Diana, was born in 1855 in Wisconsin. He was the last of the Edwards family to arrive in Westminster Colony in November 1874. He married Julia Penhall, whose father was Uriah Penhall, another colony pioneer. In 1882, he purchased a ranch where he grew crops and raised livestock. He was later a director of the Home Telephone Company in Smeltzer as well as the Bolsa Tile Factory. Later in life, he moved to Santa Ana, where he died in 1943.

Robert "Ed" Larter was 15 when he arrived in Westminster Colony in 1876 from Ontario, Canada, with his parents, Robert and Mary Jane. In 1889, he married Pearl Kiefhaber, whose father was the first blacksmith in the village. They had two daughters, Marie (who later married Orel Hare) and Lutie. Ed was a farmer and prospered by investing in celery in Smeltzer and later in real estate. He was involved with the Republican Party in Orange County during most of his adult years. He was the first resident of Westminster to be elected to the Orange County Board of Supervisors, serving from 1899 to 1902.

In 1878, a split occurred in the Presbyterian community, and in July, the Congregational church was organized. Westminster's second church followed the first built in the colony by the Methodists in 1876. It had a spire that reached 86 feet, the highest point in the village at that time. Several prominent families joined the new church, including the Andersons, the Lymans, and the Taylors. Rev. George Mack became the superintendent of the Sunday school. Along with the demise of the Grange and the closing of the Westminster Cooperative Store, this fracture contributed to Rev. Robert Strong's decision to resign as superintendent of the colony the following year.

The Reverend George C. Mack and his wife, Susan Fisher, were married in 1853. They left Solano County near the San Francisco Bay Area and arrived in Westminster Colony in 1875 with their daughter Stella. George was the first head of the newly formed Grange and an important figure in the community. Their home was moved across the street from its original site on Bolsa Avenue to make way for the Peek Funeral Home at Westminster Memorial Park.

The Westminster Cooperative Store opened in September 1874. One hundred shares in the colony's first store were sold for $25 a share. It quickly became the center of the emerging village. Shopping and farming supplies were now locally available. A month after its opening, William McPherson was elected president and Samson Edwards elected treasurer. Thomas Hull was elected manager and maintained that position until he and F.A. Lund bought it out in 1879. Hull had arrived in Westminster in 1874 and was its postmaster. As the Alward Brothers store began to prosper, Hull sold out and moved to Santa Ana, where he started a new store. (Courtesy University of California Irvine Special Collections and Archives.)

Dr. Alvin Howe and his wife, Willella, arrived in Westminster in July 1875. Six months later, he opened Westminster's first pharmacy. Soon after, Howe took over the duties of writing Westminster's annals from Walter Poor. Howe was a respected doctor in the settlement, and he and his wife taught at the school in Bolsa. They left Westminster in 1880 and moved to Chicago, where he graduated from Hahnemann Medical College a year later. They then moved to Santa Ana, where he built up a successful practice and became Santa Ana's second mayor. He moved to San Francisco in 1890, returning for family visits during the early 1890s. He became a resident surgeon at the Marine Hospital and died in San Francisco in 1904. (Courtesy Santa Ana Historical Preservation Society.)

Willella Howe graduated from the same school as her husband, Alvin, five years after him. She divorced her husband in 1897 and married Edwin Waffle in Santa Ana a year later. She went on to become one of the most prominent early women physicians in Orange County. She practiced for 38 years and delivered an estimated 1,000 babies. She passed away while on duty at a hospital in Santa Ana in 1924. (Courtesy Santa Ana Historical Preservation Society.)

Richard T. Harris's family moved to Westminster Colony in 1877 when he was 18 years old. He married in 1888 and lived in nearby Garden Grove. Harris was a rancher, a constable, a respected Westminster businessman, and an assistant postmaster and started one of the village's first telephone companies. He was the first sheriff in newly formed Orange County, serving from 1889 to 1891. He died in 1911.

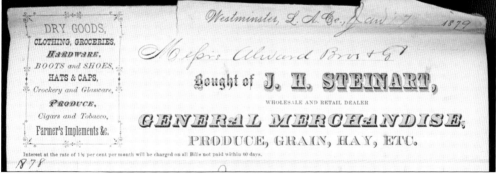

Joseph Steinart and his wife and son moved to Westminster in 1878. According to colonist Neeta Marquis, the Steinarts were the first Jewish residents of the colony. He bought out the Alward Brothers store and constructed a new house behind the building. The couple had a daughter in 1879 in Westminster. In September 1881, a fire of unknown origin destroyed their store and inventory while Steinart was in San Diego. By March 1882, they had moved to Downey. (Courtesy Huntington Library, San Marino, California.)

Five years after the death of the colony's founder, Reverend Webber, the Presbyterian church was built in 1879 at the corner of Olive Street and Plaza Street. Prior to this, the church had been meeting upstairs at the Westminster Cooperative Store. It was the third church to be built in the village, following the Methodists and Congregationalists. Rev. John Marquis, who had first organized the church in Westminster with Reverend Webber and Reverend Strong, donated the pulpit. It was built at a cost of $3,410, all of which was donated by church members.

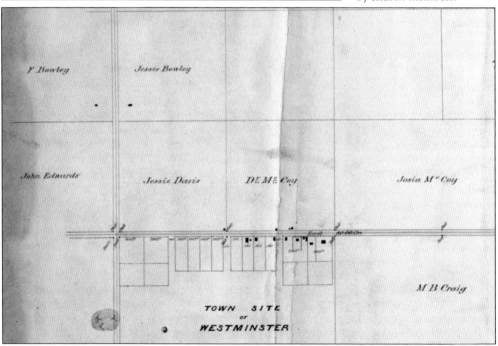

As the colony era drew to a close in 1879, the Los Angeles Assessor's Office drew this second map of Westminster Road (now Westminster Boulevard). The village center had formed near the intersection of Olive Street and Westminster Boulevard (left of center). On the southern side of the road was a hotel, the post office, Hall and Lund's store (formerly the cooperative), Steinart's store, a blacksmith shop, and a few houses. McCoy's Pharmacy was on the northern side of the road just east of Olive Street. (Courtesy Huntington Library, San Marino, California.)

Two

POST-COLONY SETTLEMENT
1881–1900

By 1880, the original tract of Westminster Colony was completely sold and occupied. After the end of the colony period, the village consisted of three churches, a school, a post office, three general merchandise stores, two blacksmiths, a wagon shop, a harness shop, and a few other enterprises. During the next decade, a saloon was established despite local protest. The price of land was between $20 and $40 an acre. The rapid growth of the first decade had come to an end with the dissolution of the colony, and the settlement's population remained virtually unchanged for the next 20 years.

Former superintendent Robert Strong continued to promote the settlement as it further developed its agricultural success. According to Strong, there were about 250 artesian wells in Westminster at this time, and the water supply was considered an advantage. Ranches, with a few exceptions, were small, ranging from 40 to 160 acres. Farms and land were consistently bought, sold, and leased. Already, real estate could be a successful endeavor in Westminster.

But industry was still sparse; a few sorghum mills produced molasses, and Robert Eccles and Samson Edwards established pork-processing businesses. The failure of Anaheim Landing as a reliable shipping point for produce was a troubling disappointment for growers. Coupled with the lack of nearby access to the railroad, these challenges forced local farmers to adapt. Drainage was also an issue, and sugar beets were found to thrive in local soil despite the alkali found in lower areas. Wheat, barley, corn, and a variety of other crops were cultivated.

With a ready market in Los Angeles, dairying became a widespread occupation. Westminster Farmers Creamery and another creamery in Bolsa were built during the 1890s. The former, following the spirit of colony pioneers, was a cooperative effort owned and operated by the local dairy farmers. Dairying would remain an important business in Westminster until the suburban era of the post–World War II period.

A ready water supply was one of the driving forces in turning the Westminster area into an agricultural center in western Orange County. During the colony period, there were around 250 wells in Westminster, and virtually every farm in Westminster had at least one well. During this period, some wells were left uncapped. Ponds and small lakes formed, attracting large flocks of geese and ducks, making Westminster a sportsman's paradise. However, roads became flooded, and travelers avoided Westminster on their way to and from Anaheim Landing until laws were enforced and the practice ended.

Westminster's second schoolhouse was the first of three to be built on the northeast corner of Hoover Street and Westminster Boulevard. Built during the early 1880s, it featured a small summer lath house nearby, part of which can be seen on the right. This was sometimes used as a setting for class photographs. This was the first school newly arriving Mexican students attended during the 1910s. It was torn down in 1915 and replaced by a landmark brick schoolhouse.

Elijah C. Phelps, left, was born in New York in 1838 and farmed tobacco in Massachusetts until he and his wife, Helen, decided to move to California. They settled in Westminster in 1884 from Selma, California, where their son Edward had been born two years earlier. Elijah is pictured above with his son Arthur (right) and William Morrill (center) during the first decade of the 20th century. The post office was located on the south side of Westminster Boulevard west of Olive Street during this period. Elijah Phelps passed away in 1924 and is buried at Magnolia Memorial Park in Garden Grove.

The Bolsa Grande School, built in 1888, replaced the former schoolhouse, which needed repairs. In 1895, the name of the district and school were shortened to Bolsa School District. The school was at the crossroads of the tiny settlement of Bolsa, on the northeast corner of Brookhurst Street and Bolsa Avenue. The school drew students from a wide area of farmland in the surrounding area. The enrollment (90–100), number of teachers (two), and funds available from the county for this school were closely equivalent to those of the Westminster School. (Courtesy Orange County Archives.)

Planting trees around their new homes was popular with early Westminster pioneers and settlers. The Phelps couple owned three homes as well as a successful feed and grain store. Before and after the turn of the 20th century, Elijah Phelps was actively engaged in real estate brokerage in the area. Elijah Phelps passed away in 1924, followed by his wife, Adelia, a year later. They are buried at Magnolia Memorial Park in Garden Grove.

As agriculture began to develop, Westminster's farmers experimented with various crops. Original settler John Anderson planted millet seed he brought from Virginia, and he quickly met with success. He built a sorghum mill and produced thousands of gallons of syrup each year. Visible on the left in this photograph is Westminster's first school building, which was moved to his farm. Anderson bought it during the 1890s and moved it to his property on Jackson Street.

Euphrates and Amy (Copeland) Hare, shown here around 1890 with their son, Orel, and a niece, arrived in Westminster in 1908. Euphrates was a blacksmith when they married in Kansas in 1883. Orel was born there two years later. They moved to Blaine, Washington, in 1891, where Hare set up a bicycle repair shop and made tools and equipment for the fishing industry. In 1908, they moved from Los Angeles to Westminster, where he set up a blacksmith shop with his son. Euphrates Hare died in 1908, and Amy Hare passed away in 1944.

WESTMINSTER, LOS ANGELES CO. CAL.

This bird's-eye view rendering of Westminster is from a promotional pamphlet in 1888. It is a good representation of the look of Westminster's agricultural community with its farms scattered around a village center. Looking southeast, Westminster Boulevard is in the lower right corner running from the lower margin to the right edge of the picture. The Congregationalist, Methodist, and Presbyterian churches are across the street from the Plaza, now called Sigler Park. In the middle of the Plaza stands the schoolhouse. Visible on the south side of Westminster Boulevard are a market, a feed and grain store, a hotel, and the Samson Edwards residence. (Courtesy Santa Ana Library.)

Briggs
Lompoc, Cal.

Leaora Blakey was born in 1891 in Lompoc, California. Encouraged by the success of the Vineland Temperance Colony in New Jersey, near Reverend Webber's birthplace, it was developed as one of the few temperance colonies in California. Blakey and her parents moved to Westminster during the early 1900s. She remained there until her death, upon which she passed on the deed to her property to the Westminster Historical Society and the city. The Leaora Blakey Historical Park and Westminster Museum are located on her former property.

Original settlers John and Virginia Anderson had two children in their two-room cabin on Monroe Street before they purchased and added on one of the school buildings at the Plaza (now Sigler Park). When the buildings were scheduled to be demolished in 1955, Walter Knott showed an interest in them and reportedly moved them to Knott's Berry Farm. John and Virginia's son Harry and his wife, Gladys, moved from their home to Santa Ana.

Oren and Stella (Mack) Byram were the children of two devoutly religious colonist families. The Mack and Byram homes were near Bolsa Avenue and Beach Boulevard, and the families were close neighbors. Stella's father, Presbyterian minister George Mack, was a respected early member of the colony who participated in the Congregationalist split from the Presbyterians in Westminster during the late 1870s. Stella, a Methodist, embraced her husband's faith when they were married in 1891. The couple had six children, one of whom fought in the First World War and another who became a missionary in Korea.

33

Memorials for Frances Willard, the head of the Women's Christian Temperance movement, were held nationwide in 1898. A memorial in the first Presbyterian church building featured her portrait (center) and the organization's banner (right). Temperance was still a powerful force in Westminster. The political influence of this movement was growing in Orange County around this time.

The Westminster Creamery was built by J.F. Halstead and a partner, both located in South Pasadena. Seven months after it opened in 1891, a group of local ranchers bought it and formed a cooperative. Patrons were stockholders, and the plant thrived. By 1893, it was shipping 1,500 pounds of butter a week to Los Angeles. Its continued success enabled it to purchase another boiler and separator in 1900. The creamery was purchased by local farmer Jacob Walton in 1902. In 1904, there was a boiler accident, and it closed shortly after.

Rachel Hickox Abbott was born in Illinois in 1863. She met her husband, George, from Missouri, in Fallbrook, California, and they moved to Santa Ana in 1889. In 1895, they bought a 10-acre ranch on Goldenwest Street and settled in Westminster. They moved to a house on the corner of Hoover Street and Westminster Boulevard. This house was torn down when the railroad was built in 1909. They then resided in the Skelly house just north of Westminster Boulevard, near Olive Street. George was Westminster's postmaster from 1906 until 1932, when he was succeeded by Clyde Day. Their daughter Nellie was Westminster's second librarian. Rachel passed away in 1922, followed by her husband 13 years later.

In 1889, David Smeltzer invested in tule land at $10 an acre two miles south of Westminster. The district, at the present-day site of Bella Terra at Edinger Avenue and Beach Boulevard, was known as Smeltzer. It soon became a thriving hub of the celery industry. A telephone exchange was established, and many Westminster ranchers invested in the area during this period. Smeltzer was shipping out 1,200 cars of celery per season and bringing in $300,000 a year. "The Celery King" passed away in 1901 at the age of 49. (Courtesy Orange County Archives.)

The Westminster Cooperative Store on what is now Westminster Boulevard, near Olive Street, was used as a post office until 1879, when Westminster's first post office was built. Dr. Foster E. Wilson was postmaster in Westminster from 1897 until 1901. In 1900, he decided to build a new post office to replace the one shown in the photograph. Wilson was a vice president of the Orange County Medical Association during the 1890s. He later moved his residence and practice to Huntington Beach.

Three

A NEW CENTURY
1901–1929

As in the rest of Orange County, a surge of settlers arrived during the 1890s, and by 1900, the village's population reached 1,590. The new century introduced progress at an accelerated rate, and Westminster transitioned from a village to a town of nearly 15,000 people by 1930.

While the village center remained relatively unchanged, electrical and telephone poles began to line Almond Street (later Westminster Boulevard) shortly after the century's first decade. Automobiles and gas stations began to make an appearance. The Smeltzer Telephone Company opened a local office in 1907. The long-awaited railroad depot opened the same year. A new brick school was built in 1915. During the same year, Willis Warner became the first superintendent of the newly formed Westminster Drainage District, finally addressing an issue that had not been previously well managed. One of the first branches of the Orange County Public Library would be built in Sigler Park almost a decade later.

When the Southern Pacific Railroad finished the spur that ran south to Westminster to Smeltzer in 1909, it finally provided growers local access to shipping. Station and postmaster John Patterson became an important figure during this transitional period. Southern Pacific provided houses for the Mexican workers who were laying and maintaining the track. These workers and their families were the origin of the Olive Street community near the Plaza (later Sigler Park).

During the 1920s, developers began to show interest in areas well outside the old village center. New communities sprang up in Midway City, Barber City, and New Westminster, where a phone exchange was built. Sterling Price and the Post brothers developed some industry in the small agricultural hamlet of Bolsa at Brookhurst Street and Bolsa Avenue. But the Depression put a rapid halt to this short era of unprecedented growth, investment, and development in the area.

The segregation of Mexican students was first introduced into the Westminster School District when a school bond was passed and the Hoover School was built on Olive Street in 1928. Westminster's second school would remain segregated until the pivotal *Mendez et al. v. Westminster School District* decision in 1947.

Westminster's association with fraternal organizations originated with the Grange during the colony days. With its demise, other groups like the Independent Order of Foresters took its place as important community organizations where business contacts could be made. In 1900, the Independent Order of Odd Fellows built a sizable two-story structure on the north side of Westminster Boulevard at Illinois Street. The Odd Fellows Hall served both as a meeting place for local groups and a landmark in what was then the center of town. It fell into disrepair and was demolished in 1964. (Courtesy First American Mortgage, Santa Ana, California.)

John Patterson was born in West Virginia in 1851 and went to Heald's Business College in San Francisco. He moved to Westminster during the late 1880s and shortly afterward opened his first store and married Virginia Carlyle Patterson. Virginia came from a family of original colonists. He was the settlement's postmaster from 1895 to 1897. Shortly after the turn of the 20th century, Wells Fargo began installing telephones in Westminster, and as the company's local agent, Patterson received the first one. He donated property for a right-of-way for the Southern Pacific Railroad to build the Westminster spur. He became the railroad's agent late in 1907 and sold tickets and handled freight. Patterson was a highly respected figure in Westminster during his lifetime.

This photograph from around 1911 depicts a visit from the Anaheim Merchants Association to the Odd Fellows Hall on the north side of Westminster Boulevard. The hall, on the left, was built in 1900 and was a meeting place for the community. In the middle is Euphrates Hare's blacksmith shop. Hare had recently moved from Blaine, Washington, with his wife, Alice, and their son, Orel. The family would remain a prominent presence in the town until the death of Orel's son, Bud, in Mexico in 1983. On the far right is the pharmacy building constructed by Dr. James McCoy in 1874. This building still stands and is located at the Leaora Blakey Historical Park in Westminster. (Courtesy Orange County Archives.)

Teacher Mabel Dickey graduated from Santa Ana High School in 1898. Like several other teachers in the area, she graduated from the Los Angeles Normal School for teachers in 1900 before taking a position in Westminster. She taught in Westminster until she married Wells B. McCoy, the son of Judge Josiah McCoy, in 1906 and left teaching shortly afterward. Wells and Mabel McCoy resided in Westminster until 1941, when they moved to Fontana.

1900   First load of sugar beets hauled by Charley Parr.
Picture contributed by Mattie Addington

Charles Parr and his wife, Nellie, were sugar beet farmers in Westminster during the first two decades of the 20th century. Nellie was the daughter of longtime Westminster postmaster George Abbott and his wife, Rachel. From 1908 until its demolition in 1921, the Parrs resided in one of the oldest homes in Westminster. It had been built in 1875 about half a mile north of the village center. In 1920, Parr was elected trustee of the Westminster School District. The Parrs spent their later years in Smeltzer.

Oren and Stella Byram's children pose in front of their house near Beach Boulevard and Bolsa Avenue in 1904. From left to right are Wilbur, Glenn, Marjorie (holding Fern), Carroll, and Roy. They were the grandchildren of colony pioneers Aaron and Harriet Byram. Carroll would die in 1917 in a railroad accident while serving in the Army during World War I.

Standing in front of the home Reverend Webber built for his family, Arthur and Bertha Fogler display large pumpkins grown on their farm. Arthur was born in 1873 in Illinois, and Bertha, born in 1875, came from Tennessee. They were married in 1896 and are shown with their two daughters. Later, they would move to Santa Ana, where Arthur continued to farm with his brother. Bertha passed away in 1947, followed by Arthur in 1951. Both are buried at Westminster Memorial Park.

Regulation of drainage and water in Westminster is reflected in this photograph taken three years after the formation of the Westminster Water District in 1915. This followed an earlier failed attempt by local residents to get the district recognized by the county. This artesian well was located west of Springdale Street and south of Garden Grove Boulevard.

J.J. Goetz was principal of the Westminster School for a few years during the middle of the first decade of the 20th century. During 1906, he and three other teachers handled classes at the school. His salary was $95 a month. In 1907, he moved on to Alamitos School, where he continued to teach. Goetz revisited Westminster in 1930 when he attended the 25th-anniversary reunion of Westminster School's 1905 graduating class.

Harry Anderson, the son of Westminster's first settlers, John and Virginia Anderson, was born in Westminster in 1878. He and his wife, Gladys, married in 1905 and resided in his parents' original house on Monroe Street. They farmed a 35-acre tract that was part of his parents' original ranch. When the library opened in Sigler Park, Gladys was its first librarian. In 1905, Harry became the treasurer of the Presbyterian church, a position he would hold for decades. H.B. Anderson School in nearby Garden Grove is named after him.

By 1907, the Presbyterian church on Olive Street had become the religious and social center of the community. It had 124 members, nine of whom were newly married Japanese Christians. In 1909, the manse was built for the residing pastor and his family next door to the Lossing home. Six years later, this original building would be replaced after a fire believed to be due to faulty wiring.

After John Warne settled in Bolsa in 1900, he soon developed 60 acres into well-irrigated farmland. He had three wells, cement pipe and open ditches, and an "up to date" pumping system in the pump house behind the ranch house. The Warne family continued to operate the farm at Bushard Street and Bolsa Avenue after John's death. When it was sold for development during the early 1980s, it was widely considered the last big farm remaining in the Bolsa area.

During the first decade of the 20th century, George Murdock's successful onion farm was located at the present site of the Westminster Civic Center. It became the headquarters for the California Seed Growers Company. Each year, Murdock hired a group of about 12 young women to clean onion sets. This group was called "The Onion Girls," and once a year, they would climb aboard a wagon and go house to house serenading local residents. In 1907, the group included Bessie and Frances Edwards, Molly Warner, and Leaora Blakey, all members of settler families.

Leaora Blakey (in the hammock on the porch) settled in Westminster with her parents when she was 14. After her father's death, she continued to live with her mother. Their home was destroyed during the 1933 Long Beach earthquake and again by fire 11 years later. She worked at various occupations, including with the Red Cross and in the defense industry during World War II. She was also a correspondent for the *Santa Ana Blade* and later for the *Santa Ana Register*.

Reuben and Adelaide (Barnes) Blakey were married in Santa Barbara in 1889. Reuben had lived, farmed, and ranched in various places in Los Angeles County prior to that. After the birth of their daughter Leaora in Lompoc in 1890, the family moved to Bolsa. They continued to live in various places in Southern California until finally settling in Westminster in 1904. They purchased the property originally owned by colonist Rev. S.B. King. King had followed Reverend Webber as pastor of the Presbyterian church in Westminster. This property is the site of one of the earliest wells drilled in the community. The Blakeys farmed and raised chickens until Reuben's death in 1914. Adelaide passed away in Westminster in 1934.

Nelson Thomas Edwards was the sixth and last son of Samson and Diane Edwards. His parents brought him to Westminster Colony when he was two years old, and he graduated from the Westminster School in 1887. He worked for his brother John's meat business and moved to Orange in 1894. He married May Tetzlaff in 1896 and had a successful meat market of his own at the Orange Plaza. He was later a director of the National Bank of Orange, the county clerk, and a member of the Orange County Board of Supervisors from 1919 to 1922. (Courtesy Orange County Archives.)

While the Presbyterian church regrouped after its split, the smaller group of Methodist pioneers and settlers continued to practice their faith. William Morrill, shown here with a Sunday school class, was an active member of the church. Morrill went into the hardware store business with John Lossing for a few years during this period. In 1912, he moved his family to Garden Grove, where he accepted a position in Keeler's Store.

Marie L. Hare was born in 1890 to original colonists Robert "Ed" and Pearl Larter. She attended the Los Angeles Normal School, where she graduated in 1910 from the general professional course in teaching. In 1912, she married Orel Hare, and they purchased their home, adding it onto the former McCoy's Pharmacy on the north side of Westminster Boulevard at Olive Street. The Hares had two children, Mary Lou and Orel Jr. or "Bud." Marie taught at the Westminster School and served as principal for 26 years at a school in Garden Grove later named after her. She donated the two buildings that comprised her family's home upon her death in 1975, and today, they stand at the Blakey Historical Park and Museum in Westminster.

The Westminster spur along Hoover Street was completed by the Southern Pacific Railroad in 1908, and this photograph shows the first train to use the newly laid line. Westminster's problem of transporting produce from a local source was finally addressed. The arrival of Mexican laborers who laid and maintained the tracks and lived in housing built by Southern Pacific marked the first development of their community on nearby Olive Street and the area surrounding Sigler Park.

The long-awaited combination passenger and freight railroad depot finally arrived in November 1907. It was built at a cost of $4,800 and was located a few hundred yards north of Westminster Boulevard, west of the tracks along Hoover Street. It was a standard, single-story, No. 23 Southern Pacific depot without living quarters. Its main purpose was to transport local sugar beets and celery from the Smeltzer area. Suddenly, travel time to Los Angeles was a little more than an hour for passengers.

Blacksmith Charles Bauer and his wife, Ethel, moved to Westminster from Anaheim around 1903, three years after they married. Bauer moved his shop from Anaheim to Westminster Boulevard, where he practiced blacksmithing and wagon making. In 1907, the couple lost an infant daughter. That same year, they acquired ranch property in Rancho Cucamonga. The ranch had 15 acres of navel oranges, which prospered, and they soon moved there.

Westminster Boulevard, initially named Almond Street, was still unpaved when Ethel Bauer posed in her buggy looking eastward near Olive Street. The Odd Fellows Hall on the street behind her dominated the still sparsely developed north side of the main street. The McCoy's Pharmacy building is hidden behind her, and Hare's Garage would be constructed next to it during the next few years.

Westminster's reputation for being an agriculturally productive area in the county was well established by the beginning of the 20th century. Orange County's Parade of Products was held in downtown Santa Ana in October 1908. Westminster was included in a division along with Fullerton, Anaheim, Orange, and El Toro. Its float was especially noted by onlookers. Called "The Artesian Belt Float," it featured a replica of a burbling, partially capped well pipe. It also displayed produce grown in peat-bog soil considered especially rich. (Courtesy Orange County Archives.)

John and Addie (Kiefhaber) Lossing, with their daughter, Mildred, moved into their home at 14051 Olive Street in 1907, shortly after it was built. Lossing was president of the Smeltzer Home Telephone Company in 1907 and owned a restaurant on Westminster Boulevard. For about six months in 1909, they had a small ostrich farm behind the house. The family moved the ostriches to Sanger, California, and followed them there in 1912. John, Addie, and Mildred are buried side by side in Sanger.

Charles and Minnie McCall moved to California from Iowa in 1910. Charles was originally from Missouri, and Minnie was a teacher in Iowa before they decided to relocate. They arrived in Westminster in 1912 and purchased the home of Sylvester and Nettie Lyman, located on Beach Boulevard north of Trask Avenue. They lived there for two years, during which their daughter Fay was born. The McCalls later built a home on the corner of Sixteenth Street and Cedarwood Street, where they lived until Minnie's death in 1953. Charles passed away 10 years later.

Originally from Minnesota, Lyman Toogood brought his family to Westminster in 1907. His wife, Lylia, was the sister of Ed Finley's wife, Amelia. They owned property in Los Angeles and farmed and raised chickens. They moved to Long Beach in 1918. In 1920, they sold their home in Westminster and a rooming house in Los Angeles and moved to Missouri. They spent their later years in San Diego.

The elderly William "W.W." Baker and his wife, Eliza, moved to Westminster in 1891. They arrived from Santa Ana, where their son Dan was the editor of the *Santa Ana Standard*. In 1891, W.W. purchased a tract of land that was called Baker's Addition on Westminster Boulevard. It remained in his family after his death in 1895. The house still stands on Cherry Street. Nearby Iowa Street was named after the state the family regarded as second home.

Joshua and Flora Pyle settled in Westminster during the mid-1880s. Joshua was one of the directors of the Westminster Creamery in 1892. He hauled the lumber used to build the Odd Fellows Hall and was the treasurer of the Odd Fellows when it was formed in 1900. The family's 46-foot-by-60-foot home on Hoover Street between Westminster Boulevard and Hazard Avenue was built in 1908. The Mission-style house was designed by Flora. Josh died in 1940, followed by Flora 12 years later. They are buried at Westminster Memorial Park.

By the time a Mrs. Reagan, the proprietress of the Reagan Hotel on Westminster Boulevard, moved to Fresno with her children in 1914, there were several landmark buildings in the village center that would characterize it for the next four decades. Seen on the left side of the street are the post office, the Odd Fellows Hall, Hare's Garage, and the pointed roof of McCoy's old drugstore. On the right is the hotel and, past the car, Patterson's store at Olive Street.

Samson Edwards's auction notice in a Santa Ana newspaper in 1905 illustrates the diverse efforts on his successful ranch. Horses and livestock such as dairy cattle, pigs, hogs, and horses are mentioned for sale. Corn, barley, and oats were a few of the crops he cultivated. Edwards championed planting eucalyptus trees, and he also offered eight cords of the wood that was 25 years old. (Courtesy University of California Irvine Special Collections and Archives.)

AUCTION

Having sold my stock ranch 2½ miles southwest of Westminster, I will sell at Public Auction

THURSDAY, OCTOBER 26th

20 head No. 1 Milch Cows, 1 Durham Bull, 4 years old, 1 Jersey Bull, 1 year old, 9 yearling heifers, 5 heifer calves, 2 brood sows, 11 pigs, a number of stock hogs, 1 large Berkshire boar, one 5-year-old brood mare and colt, one bay colt three years old, three work horses and three sets of double harness, one double disc plow nearly new, one two-horse wagon, two sulky plows, two harrows, one drum roller, one corn sheller, one mower, one hay rake, one 2-horse walking plow, one 1-horse bar plow, one double-shovel plow, one Stockton Gang plows 20 tons baled barley and oat hay, 200 feet picket fence, one fence machine, one spray pump large kettle, one cross-cut s w, 8 cords gum wood of 25 years' growth, lot of hog fence panels, one disc harrow—nearly new, six milk cans and other articles too numerous to mention.

Sale Will Commence Promptly at Ten O'clock.

Lunch Will Be Served on the Grounds

TERMS OF SALE—All sums of $20 and under, cash; over $20, a credit of six months without interest. Purchaser to give bankable note, or note with approved security satisfactory to the owner of the aforesaid goods.

J. W. STUCKENBRUCK, AUCTIONEER

SAMSON EDWARDS OWNER

Thomas Hosack (seated center) was principal of the Westminster School from 1908 to 1917. Among those in the group around him are original colonist descendants Raymond Penhall (far right), Marjorie Bynam (standing next to Penhall), and Charles Walton (standing center). Hosack moved with his wife to La Habra to fill a teaching position there until 1922, when they returned to Westminster. In 1924, he formed a realty company with Ed Larter, which was fairly successful. The Hosacks were active members of the Presbyterian church.

During the mid-1910s, Orel and Euphrates Hare bought a city block in Westminster and expanded the original blacksmith shop to include auto repairs. The shop was located on the north side of Westminster Boulevard at Olive Street. The transition from repairing farm equipment to automobiles was a natural one for Orel. His son Bud's interests would later develop in a similar way, moving from blacksmith and auto mechanic to engineering and racing motorcycles. To the left of them is the first gas pump in Westminster.

By 1918, the village center at Westminster Boulevard and Olive Street was well established. The north side (right) of Westminster Boulevard featured the two-story landmark Odd Fellows Hall, Hare's Garage, and the building that housed McCoy's Pharmacy from colony days. On the south side (left) was Patterson's store, a drugstore, and a hotel, along with other businesses. The road was paved during the mid-1910s.

The brick schoolhouse, built in 1915, was the second school constructed on the northeast corner of Hoover Street and Westminster Boulevard. It was designed by architect J. Flood Walker and built at a cost of $15,000. The building measured 105 feet by 63 feet. It housed Westminster's library before it was moved from there to a new building in Sigler Park. Damage from the 1933 Long Beach earthquake resulted in its demolition, and it was replaced at the same site by the Seventeenth Street School. (Courtesy First American Mortgage, Santa Ana, California.)

Mexican students began to appear alongside white students in class photographs during the 1910s. Posing on the steps of the brick schoolhouse are a Miss Knoll's first- and second-grade classes in 1917. Classes remained integrated until the Hoover School was built in 1929. Clyde Day, shown in the first row at far right, would later become Westminster's postmaster.

In 1903, the Westminster School Board elected John Lossing as president and E.C. Phelps as secretary. The teachers were I.H. Chapman, Mary McCoy, and Mabel Dickey. A fourth teacher, Lena Sprague, served for a short period before suffering a nervous breakdown. Included in this photograph is graduate Marie Larter Hare, whose father was Orange County supervisor Ed Larter. She would go on to become a longtime and recognized local educator.

Penhall Garage opened in 1926 on the south side of Westminster Boulevard near Chestnut Street. It was operated by Francis and Merton Penhall, had a 50-foot lathe and presses, and served as the headquarters for the family's successful trucking company. Soon, the Penhalls would open a service station in Midway City, where Leslie built a small airplane. Later, in the 1930s, another Penhall service station opened in Brawley.

The Penhall Brothers Trucking Company began operating in the mid-1910s. The company delivered cream to Los Angeles and later drove gasoline trucks in Southern California. Brothers Francis, Raymond, and Merton Penhall are seen sitting from left to right in the driver seats. Their father, Harry, is on the right with their brother Leslie (far right). At the age of six, Harry arrived in Westminster in 1872 with his parents.

John Warne was born in England in 1870 to a farming family and immigrated to the United States at the age of 17. He came to California during the 1890s, residing and finding farmwork in Hanford for eight years. He finally settled in Bolsa, where he bought property and built a farmhouse at the corner of Brookhurst and Bushard Streets. In 1905, he married Sarah McGarvin, who was born in Orange County and raised in Garden Grove. Warne's descendants later donated the farmhouse and barn to the Westminster Historical Museum.

In 1922, John Harper purchased and subdivided 200 acres at the northeast section of Beach Boulevard and Bolsa Avenue. A year later (the year of this view looking east), he began selling lots in what he called Midway City. During the following years, a small community formed, made up mainly of oil workers in Huntington Beach and their families. This early settlement had close ties with Westminster but became its own community fairly quickly.

Helena Dimock began teaching at Westminster School in 1920. She lived half a mile east of Smeltzer and retired in the late 1920s. Included in this photograph of her diverse class are Mexican, Japanese, and white children. Future motorcycle legend Bud Hare is in the top row, second student from the left.

Dr. Roy Byram was a grandson of colony pioneers Aaron and Harriet Byram. He and his wife, Dr. Bertha Stanley Byram, met at Occidental College in Los Angeles during the late 1910s. They became Presbyterian missionaries and spent 20 years in Korea until they were imprisoned by the Japanese for two years during World War II. After their release, they returned to Westminster and remained there until they passed away, Bertha in 1964 and Roy in 1974.

The Barber City Women's Club was founded by Irma Foster, an ex-schoolteacher, in 1927. At that time, it was called the Barber City Women's Improvement League, and its purpose was to facilitate improvements and development in the newly built community. In 1931, the club joined the Orange District Federation of Women's Clubs and dropped "Improvement" from its name. During the 1950s and until 1963, the building was a branch of the Orange County Public Library and served this purpose until its collection was absorbed by the new Westminster Branch. (Courtesy Orange County Archives.)

The first annual Old Settlers Reunion was held at Anaheim Landing in 1917. It changed locations in 1925, moving to the Presbyterian church and hall on Olive Street, where it continued to be held until the middle of the Second World War. A wealth of Westminster lore, memories, and oral histories were shared at these reunions. Colonist families represented in this photograph from the mid-1920s are the Byrams, the Macks, the Larters, the Kiefhabers, the Craigs, and the Rogers.

In 1926, a reception was held at the Presbyterian church honoring the missionary work in Korea of Drs. Roy and Bertha Byram. As an unannounced addition to the proceedings, there was a wedding between Roy's sister Fern and Dudley Smith, and Roy joined the wedding party. Two of the Smiths' children would go on to become missionaries.

Previous to 1927, Westminster's library had been housed at the Westminster School on Hoover Street and Westminster Boulevard before the collection moved to the Odd Fellows Hall. Westminster's first library building was constructed in Sigler Park in early 1927. The design incorporated ideas from the new Placentia Library and cost $1,200, with some of the work being donated by residents. The stucco, cream-colored, 32-foot-by-26-foot library opened in November 1928. The Westminster Branch of the Orange County Public Library remained in this location until 1963, when it moved to the shopping center on Goldenwest Street and Westminster Boulevard. (Courtesy Orange County Archives.)

Four

DEPRESSION, WORLD WAR, AND POSTWAR

1930–1956

The Depression, which began in 1929, put a halt to what appeared to be a promising decade of development. But Westminster continued to be an agricultural and dairy center. Main crops were lima beans, sugar beets, and alfalfa. A volunteer fire department was formed in the early 1930s and operated out of Hare's Garage with Orel Hare as supervisor. The Long Beach earthquake in 1933 caused enough damage to the brick schoolhouse to require its demolition. It took several years to build a new schoolhouse, and the auditorium was not completed until 1940. This school would later be known as the Seventeenth Street School. The jazz era made a brief appearance in Westminster at the Bear Café on the corner of Goldenwest Street and Westminster Boulevard.

The town's population remained static through the Second World War. The women's clubs in Westminster, Midway City, and Barber City were especially active in support of the war effort. The internment of Japanese people began in 1942, and most of the local Japanese were sent to the camp in Poston, Arizona. Many left the area when they later returned and found their property in various stages of disrepair. A Catholic parish began organizing on Olive Street, and the first Blessed Sacrament Church was established in 1947. Servicemen stationed in Southern California were attracted to the climate, and there was modest but steady growth during the years following the war's conclusion in 1945.

In 1946, the quiet farming town became the backdrop for a court decision that would put an end to the school district's 20-year segregation era. The scope of the *Mendez v. Westminster School District* decision was limited, pertaining only to Mexican students. But its national implications concerning the future ending of segregation in schools were clear. Judge Paul McCormick's decision predated the landmark *Brown v. Board of Education* by eight years.

By the mid-1950s, Orange County's population boom reached Westminster, where housing tracts, strip malls, and shopping centers began to replace large tracts of farmland. After more than 80 years as an agricultural center, Westminster was entering a new suburban era. Surrounding towns in the county were incorporating, and Westminster would soon join them.

In May 1927, the Long Beach development company of Deeble and Chapman began work on what would soon be called New Westminster. The 80-acre tract, intended to be small chicken farms, was located northeast of the intersection of Beach Boulevard and Westminster Boulevard. A surge of growth occurred in this area as a result. Sidewalks and curbs were built at the intersection, and the drainage ditch was replaced by a pipe. Soon Southern California Edison was planning to build a substation there. The telephone company also built an exchange at this location. A two-story brick building large enough to house five businesses was constructed at a cost of $30,000. The impressive growth of this community soon came to an end with the onset of the Depression in 1929. (Courtesy Orange County Archives.)

During 1927 and 1928, the Zenith Aircraft Corporation built what was widely considered the largest plane on the West Coast. The president of the corporation was Midway City resident Sterling Price, a director of the American National Bank in Santa Ana. The Albatross was designed by Charles Rocheville and A.K. Peterson. Peterson was also involved in its construction, which took place in Midway City. It had a 90-foot wingspan and a 57-foot fuselage length. It was planned to seat nine passengers and featured a bunk for pilots during a projected 70-hour flight. The plane was completed and flew its first flight in January 1928. (Courtesy University of California Irvine Special Collections and Archives.)

In February 1928, the Albatross made a test flight with the goal of staying in flight for 70 hours. After 27 hours in the air, the three Siemens-Halske engines overheated, and the company had to cut the flight short. In 1929, Zenith was bought by Schofield Inc., and the Albatross was retooled there with three Axel-7R engines. It flew well, and plans were made to build more of the planes and provide a service to Guatemala. But with the onset of the Depression, interest was soon lost, and the projects were never realized.

During the 1920s, Westminster experienced a surge in growth, and it was decided that a new school would be built to house the growing student body. In keeping with a trend in Orange County, it would be a segregated school aimed at "Americanizing" the Mexican population. Westminster voted a year earlier for a $10,000 school bond by a vote of 97-7. The school was built on Olive Street at Maple Street at a cost of $2,000. It opened in March 1929, serving 81 Mexican pupils, while the remaining 272 white students stayed at the Westminster School on Hoover Street and Westminster Boulevard. The first principal was Hazel (Peck) Campbell, and the teachers were Myra Evans and Mary Thomason. The school reintegrated after the Mendez decision in 1947. After the city incorporated, the school was used for city hall, the council chambers, and Westminster's first police department.

During the 1930s and into the 1940s, Westminster School held an annual maypole dance to celebrate May Day. Being chosen to wind the maypole and sing was considered a privilege and honor by then fourth-grader Thelma Crouch. In 1940, students were encouraged to dress in colonial costumes for the festivities. The event appears to have been discontinued after World War II. (Courtesy Janet Filbeck.)

Midway City volunteer fireman and mechanic Jess Beavers stands with his daughter Mary Jo and his son Jerry in front of the Midway City Garage around 1930. This full-service station was located on the southwest corner of Beach Boulevard and Bolsa Avenue. Purple-colored Violet Ray gasoline was introduced by the General Petroleum Corporation in 1928. It was used by 3,500 service stations on the West Coast for a few years before being discontinued. (Courtesy Tim Castroreale.)

Grand Opening of the

BEAR CAFE

Dining

Dancing

Entertain-
ment

Excellent

Cuisine

At WESTMINSTER

Thursday Night, Sept. 1st

LOOK FOR THE SEARCHLIGHT

Irene Howard, Dancer Supreme—Harry Judson, Master of Ceremonies—Jack Nash and his band and entertainers.—Jimmie
Arnerich will greet you at the door.

OPEN EVERY NIGHT IN THE YEAR

The jazz era made a brief appearance in Westminster in 1929 when the Bear Café opened at the corner of Goldenwest Street and Westminster Boulevard. It was opened during Prohibition by two restaurant entrepreneurs from Los Angeles named Kirby and Nash. The Bear Café featured a jazz band, dancing, and relatively fine dining and had the capacity for 350 people. A newspaper article from that era describes an early and rare appearance of Black people in the town when Jim Erwing and "his colored band" appeared during its first year. During its heyday for the next two years, it became a popular spot, drawing customers from Santa Ana and Long Beach. After a couple of years, the Orange County supervisors decided to withdraw its dancing license. It struggled to survive afterward, finally closing its doors in 1933. (Courtesy University of California Irvine Special Collections and Archives.)

The Midway City Women's Club was organized in 1929 and incorporated in 1935. The 3,200-square-foot building was located at the corner of Bolsa Avenue and Monroe Street. It was built by local realtor and developer John Harper at a cost of $4,000. It was also used by the Midway City Chamber of Commerce. During World War II, it served as a USO center. It became the center of activity for the community, providing a place for meetings, benefits, and dances. It was moved to Westminster in 1959 and currently houses the Westminster Historical Museum at Leaora Blakey Park.

Born in 1907 in Bolsa to Sterling Price and Florence Heil, Gerald Price flew his first solo flight at the age of 18. He serviced bush planes in Mexico and Alaska for his father's aircraft company. In 1932, Gerald converted his father's hangar for the Albatross in Bolsa into a shop that manufactured farm equipment. His company was fairly successful locally and exported equipment as well. Gerald passed away in Stanton in 2002 at the age of 94.

During the 1930s, Orel Hare was semiretired, while his wife, Marie, continued her successful career in education. Their son, Bud, had learned to be a mechanic and was beginning to race motorcycles. They had added a few cottages on the back half of their property and built an "auto camp." In 1932, Orel became the first fire chief for the newly formed Westminster Volunteer Fire Department, and the garage became the headquarters for the department.

The Finley Corner was located on the southwest corner of Edwards Street and Westminster Boulevard. It was inherited from Samuel Finley, an early settler in Westminster, by Edward Finley. He married Amalia in 1908. He and his wife ran a gas station and feed store at this outpost toward the western edge of the settlement during the 1930s and 1940s. The Finley School was named after his family.

W.E. Moore and his wife established a dairy farm in Midway City around 1930. Moore had some success growing berries as well as other crops on his ranch. He was also active in the chamber of commerce, serving as an aide to an improvement and development committee. His wife was popular and involved in civic activities. She was the president of the Midway City Woman's Club during the 1930s. (Courtesy Orange County Archives.)

Dr. Russell Johnson had been in the Westminster–Midway City area for three years when the Long Beach earthquake struck in 1933. Brick facades and buildings did not fare well during the quake, and there was very little construction with brick in the town after that. This clinic was one of his first efforts on his way toward establishing a hospital in Westminster. Twenty-five years later, his efforts would culminate in the opening of Westminster Community Hospital.

The Long Beach earthquake in 1933 caused extensive damage there and in Orange County. Cracks a few inches wide were seen in farmland around Westminster. Brick buildings were especially vulnerable, and structural damage is evident at McDaniel's Garage. It was located on the north side of Westminster Boulevard near Chestnut Street, just west of the post office. The Odd Fellows Hall is seen in the background.

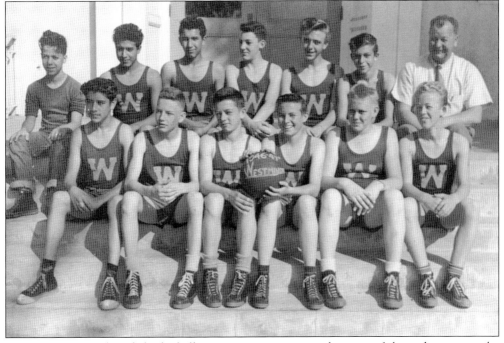

The 1946–1947 Colonials basketball team is seen posing on the steps of the auditorium at the Seventeenth Street School. The Westminster School's name underwent a change during the postwar period. This photograph was taken shortly after the *Mendez v. Westminster* decision. The coach, seated on the right, had the last name of Mitchell.

A few years after it was built, the Teepee Gas Station, at the southeast corner of Beach Boulevard and Bolsa Avenue, was leased by Midway City Garage owner Jess Beaver in 1938. Later that year, he; his wife, Thelma; and their family moved into the new residence next to the recently built Midway City Volunteer Fire Department. The residence was meant for the department's truck driver, and Beaver was the first to hold the position. The Teepee Gas Station was torn down in 1954. (Courtesy Tim Castroreale.)

The Midway City Volunteer Fire Department began forming around the same time as Westminster's in 1932. Harold Robertson was its first chief, and in 1935, the state allocated the fire department its first truck. The Midway City Volunteer Fire Department served a wide area surrounding its location on the corner of Beach Boulevard and Bolsa Boulevard. (Courtesy Tim Castroreale.)

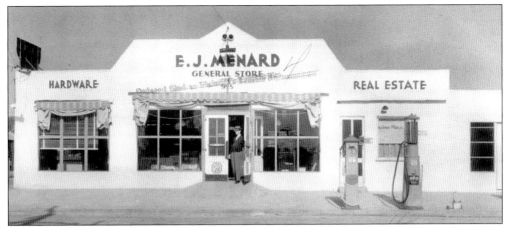

Ernest Menard's general store opened during the mid-1930s and remained operating for a short time during World War II. It was located on the north side of Westminster Boulevard, just east of Olive Street. It was also an independent Hancock service station. The Menards were Presbyterians, and his wife, Velma, was a member of the Young Matrons Club. The store later became a market before being torn down during the late 1950s. (Courtesy Orange County Archives.)

In response to the silt left on the topsoil by the flooding of the Santa Ana River in 1937, Norman and Charles "Hap" Post built what was widely considered at the time to be the world's largest plow in Bolsa. It weighed 15 tons, was 37 feet long, and had an 86-foot blade that left a six-foot-deep furrow. Pulled by five D8 Caterpillar tractors, it served the Santa Ana Valley. It was also used as far away as Ventura and Nevada. The plow is on display at the Westminster Historical Museum.

Several recognizable locations in postwar Westminster are visible in this view looking west in 1948, two years after the Mendez decision. Among them are the building that housed Lloyd Thomas's newspaper, the *Westminster Herald*; the Seventeenth Street School; the ballpark at Sigler Park; the Odd Fellows Hall; and the water tower on Wyoming Street. By this time, commercial activity was shifting to New Westminster, a mile or so to the east. (Courtesy Orange County Archives.)

From 1944 until 1946, Blessed Sacrament parishioners held weekly Sunday Jamaicas (or "little fiestas"). These fund-raising events offered craft items and traditional Mexican food and drew large crowds from as far away as Santa Ana and San Pedro. Funds from these events were donated to Fr. John McFadden for Blessed Sacrament Church.

Seven years after the Long Beach earthquake severely damaged the Westminster School, work was completed on the new building. Five classrooms, a kindergarten classroom, and an auditorium were part of a Works Progress Administration project costing over $100,000. Other intended improvements would include work on the school grounds and the construction of tennis courts. This school would later be known as the Seventeenth Street School. The auditorium was the last of the original buildings to be demolished in 1998.

Henry Akiyama had worked with goldfish for 11 years in Wintersburg before opening his Pacific Goldfish Farm in 1928. It was first located on the corner of Goldenwest Street and Westminster Boulevard and quickly expanded. In 1935, it moved to the northwest corner of Goldenwest Street and Bolsa Avenue. When Akiyama returned from internment at Poston, Arizona, during World War II, he began growing koi fish as well. This view looking northwest is from the postwar period. The goldfish farm closed in 1971, making way for the Westminster Mall. (Courtesy California State University Center for Oral and Public History.)

In 1936, Ray Schmitt bought a 10-acre farm on the corner of Beach Boulevard and Twenty-Third Street from Fred Day. He promptly built it into a dairy farm that operated successfully for the next two decades. In the early 1950s, he became a trustee for the school district, and in 1954, he was elected one of the directors of the chamber of commerce. The Ray Schmitt School on Trask Avenue is named after him.

Orel and Marie Hare's son, Bud, served as an airplane mechanic during World War II. Bud and his father's interest in motorcycles predated the war, and shortly after the war ended, his career building motorcycles began in earnest. Triumphs were ubiquitous during the postwar period, and he specialized in those. By the late 1950s, he was setting speed records at Bonneville and built what is believed to be the first dual-engine drag bike, "Dubble Trubble."

The Midway City 4-H Club was organized in 1937 by Ross Crane. The group was focused mainly on agricultural efforts, at which young resident Bob Heil excelled. He won several awards and commendations during his time in the club. He is shown here in 1941 with his father, Armand, examining his award-winning crop of popcorn. It yielded 4,700 pounds of popcorn on one acre. (Courtesy Orange County Archives.)

Westminster's newly formed volunteer fire department was housed in this station built in 1951. The firefighters included J.R. Dunham, Frank Eastwood, Glenn Young, R.F. Harris, W.E. Jolley, fire chief Mel Ingram, Stanley Janesky, future city council member Art Paysen, John Novacek, Marshall Patterson, Mert Dunham, and Henry Nordsieck. It served the department until it was torn down in 1961.

Japanese nationals Seima (right) and Masako Munemitsu leased a farm in Torrance before moving to Westminster with their two sons in 1931. With the help of Frank Monroe, a banker in Garden Grove, they purchased the 40-acre farm they were leasing on Edwards Street. Shortly after President Roosevelt signed Executive Order 9066, Seima was arrested on suspicion of being a spy and sent to Santa Fe, New Mexico, until 1943. His wife and family were sent to the incarceration camp at Poston, Arizona. Seima was "paroled" and reunited with his wife and two daughters at this camp in 1944. (Courtesy Janice Munemitsu from *The Kindness of Color*.)

The Munemitsus' sons, Lincoln "Tad" (left) and Saylo (center), worked on the farm in Westminster until the family's incarceration in 1942. The property was legally in Tad's name, as his parents were not yet US citizens. Tad would later become a businessman, and Saylo went on to become a surgeon. (Courtesy Janice Munemitsu from *The Kindness of Color*.)

While the Munemitsu family was incarcerated in Arizona, the Mendez family leased and became caretakers of their farm on Edwards Street. Gonzalo and Felicitas Mendez were in the early stages of what would become the *Mendez et al. v. Westminster School District* anti-segregation case. When the Munemitsu family returned from incarceration in Arizona in 1945, an arrangement was made for the Mendezes to live in the farmhouse. Gonzalo had retained attorney David Marcus at his own expense as the case moved forward. (Courtesy Janice Munemitsu from *The Kindness of Color*.)

Gonzalo and Felicitas Mendez married in 1935 and a few years later opened a restaurant, the Arizona Cantina, in Santa Ana. He was born in Chihuahua, Mexico, and she was born in Puerto Rico. Gonzalo was a successful businessman, and the couple purchased three houses and saved enough money to lease two farms in Westminster, where Gonzalo had grown up. (Courtesy Mendez family.)

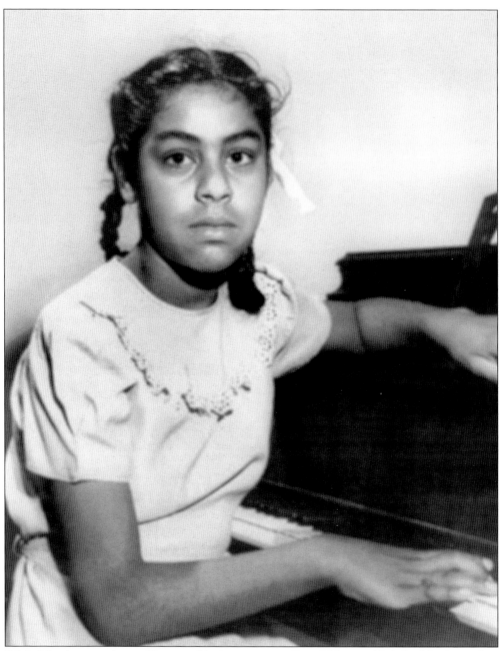

Sylvia Mendez was almost 10 years old when attorney David Marcus filed the *Mendez et al. v. Westminster School District* class action lawsuit on March 2, 1945. After a five-day trial in 1946, federal judge Paul McCormick ruled in favor of the plaintiffs, effectively ending segregation in public schools in Orange County's school districts. Westminster School District did not join the subsequent appeal, which failed two years later. Sylvia and her brothers attended Seventeenth Street School for a year before the family moved back to Santa Ana. (Courtesy Mendez family.)

In 1918, a school bond election was held in the Bolsa School District to approve a measure to raise $12,000 in order to build a new schoolhouse in Bolsa. By the fall of 1919, a new building had been constructed on the northeast corner of Brookhurst Avenue and Bolsa Avenue. Architects Jeffrey and Schaefer of Los Angeles would soon afterward build the new Talbert School. This photograph, taken in 1947, shows the segregated class at the school while the Mendez case was being appealed.

Organized by Fr. Robert Ross and members of the Olive Street community, the participants in the Westminster Fiesta parades and celebrations were fairly diverse. They included a parade with horses and riders, bands, drill teams, and wagons. In 1947, it featured an orchestra with *paso doble* flamenco dancers from a church in Boyle Heights. The annual parades and carnivals would be a precursor to the Founders Day parades that began after the city's incorporation. (Courtesy Orange County Archives.)

During World War II, the Barber City Women's Club supported the war effort with a variety of activities. Over the years, the club's building served the Girl Scouts, Brownies, Blue Birds, Campfire Girls, and Sewing Club meetings. Pictured in this photograph from the 1950s are, from left to right, (first row) Floy Hillborn, Lucille Oliphant, Edith Riley, and Minnie Upham; (second row) Florence Tyler and Isabell Crowell; (third row) Ruth Gobel and Willy Kuykendall.

Tri-City Wranglers was an equestrian club first organized in 1946 in Midway City. Dr. Russell Johnson, after whom Johnson Intermediate School is named, was an early organizer and president of the club. Its name was one of the first times "Tri-City" was used for the area that comprised Westminster, Midway City, and Barber City. The club held its first horse show in June 1948. It soon moved to a location on Edwards Street north of Westminster Boulevard, where the club built a clubhouse and corrals. The Tri-City Wranglers participated in horse shows and tournaments in Southern California and held dances at the clubhouse. In 1959, the Wranglers organized a rodeo for Westminster's Founders Day. The club disbanded not long after.

When the Blessed Sacrament Church parish began forming on Olive Street in 1947, it held the first Westminster Fiesta. It also featured an orchestra with paso doble flamenco dancers from a church in Boyle Heights. With pastor Robert Ross acting as chairman, the Westminster Fiestas became a popular annual attraction showcasing Southland equestrian groups. It was held each July in Southern California and drew remarkable crowds. They ended when Blessed Sacrament held its first Spring Festival in 1957.

Clara Cook was born in Iowa in 1891 and came to California in 1912. She began teaching in Westminster in 1932. She taught in Fullerton, Bakersfield, and Long Beach before embarking on a 24-year career at Seventeenth Street School. She taught first grade for 18 years there. She and her husband, Fred, moved to a home he built on the corner of Chestnut Street and Park Street in 1939. They had two sons and a daughter. Clara passed away a few years before Clara Cook School opened on Willow Street in 1960.

Willis Warner (right) was the manager of San Pedro Lumber Company at Hoover Street and Westminster Boulevard in 1914. In 1915, he became secretary for the newly formed Westminster Drainage District. He was elected mayor of Huntington Beach in 1936 and went on to serve on the Orange County Board of Supervisors from 1939 until 1963. He was the chairman of the board for 17 years during this period. Warner Avenue and Warner Middle School on Newland Street are named after him. (Courtesy Orange County Archives.)

Manuel Regalado poses with his Murray Pontiac station wagon at his house on Olive Street. Regalado's uncle, Feliciano Caudillo, served as a representative for the Comision Honorifica Mexicana (Mexican Honorary Commission) in Westminster during the 1930s. The commission worked as a kind of liaison between the Mexican consul and the immigrant community. (Courtesy John Regalado.)

Francis Penhall (left, with Ray Schmidt) was the grandson of original colonists Uriah and Letitia Penhall. He was born in 1892 and grew up on the Penhall ranch, located at the present site of Westminster Mall. Francis drove a dairy truck for the family business. He married Ruth Walton, and they had two sons. During the 1920s, Francis and his brother Merton opened the Penhall Brothers Garage on Westminster Boulevard. Ruth passed away in 1975, followed by Francis three years later.

In 1948, a meeting of the Barber City Chamber of Commerce was held regarding the name of the street that bordered the east side of the community. It was changed from Edwards Street to Hammon Street. Art Coopman is seen in the second row, third from the left. He and his wife, Vi, would later own the nearby Twin Palms Café. William Jolley, a civically active resident during this time, is at far right.

In 1952, the Westminster Volunteer Fire Department acquired a Chevrolet one-ton rescue panel van from Orange County. It was one of about a dozen unique panel vans designed by the county. It was equipped with a pump, small water tank, and hose that unreeled from the back. It cost a little over $5,000, much of which was raised through the Westminster Women's Club's fund-raising. In 1962, the newly formed fire department acquired it from the county and painted it white.

In April 1947, a Catholic parish was formed around the Mexican community on Olive Street under the supervision of local missionary Fr. John McFadden. Initially, the parish utilized the small church used by local Japanese farmers until they were interred during World War II. On Christmas Day in 1950, the first mass was held in a new building designed by architect Gene Verge of Los Angeles. In 1958, under the guidance of Fr. Robert Ross, two wings and a sacristy were built to accommodate the new and growing population, tripling its size.

Lorena Tringham took over librarian duties at the library in Sigler Park in September 1951. She followed Gladys Anderson, who had served for 25 years. Lorena's husband, James, was a teacher at Seventeenth Street School until 1953. He was a volunteer fireman and Boy Scout leader for Westminster's Troop 2. She kept the librarian position until May 1962.

During the early postwar period, there was an increase in local demand for postal services. In 1945, the annual postal receipts amounted to $8,000. Postmaster La Verne Strawbridge saw her staff grow from 3 to 10 employees during the following four years. Until 1949, there was a rural delivery service, but the businesses in the old village center and New Westminster had to obtain their mail at the post office. After local delivery was introduced, a building (above) was constructed on Westminster Boulevard between Cherry Street and Illinois Street. By 1960, receipts had grown to $140,000, and the post office employed 37 people, requiring the lease of a new building still in use on Goldenwest Street. (Courtesy Orange County Archives.)

The owner and editor of the sometimes locally controversial *Westminster Herald*, Lloyd Thomas moved with his parents and brother, Lynn, to the Westminster area in 1934. A year after he and his brother returned from World War II, Lynn founded the weekly community newspaper, which Lloyd soon took over. Thomas used an old-fashioned, hot lead–type printing press that was one of the last of its kind until he converted to offset printing in 2003. He passed away in 2018 and is buried in Westminster Memorial Park.

Around 1938, noted attorney and one-time director of the Long Beach Bar Association Clyde McWhinney built his home on the north side of Bolsa Avenue near Beach Boulevard. McWhinney was president of the Westminster Memorial Park Association and part owner of the property. In 1947, a year after his death, the property was sold to the Peek family. During the mid-1950s, they remodeled the interior, and Peek Family Mortuary was opened. A chapel and administrative building were added in 1959.

The Hiway 39 Drive-In, located at the northeast corner of Beach Boulevard and Trask Avenue, opened in 1955. Its screen was one of the largest in the Pacific Theater drive-in chain at that time. It expanded to four screens in 1979. The drive-in was a perennial favorite for families and a popular dating spot for young couples. It was the last of Orange County's drive-ins to show movies when it closed in 1997. Included in the drive-in's last program was *Beavis and Butthead Do America*. It was replaced by a Walmart and Eagle Hardware. (Courtesy Orange County Archives.)

Five

THE SUBURBAN ERA AND THE INCORPORATED CITY
1957–1976

By the mid-1950s, Orange County had become one big home show for realtors and prospective new home buyers. With terms attractive to veterans, housing tracts were springing up everywhere in the area, and Westminster's population, at about 26,000, was starting to surge. Strip malls and shopping centers began to appear, and the sudden need for schools and infrastructure was readily apparent. Paved roads, water supply, and drainage issues were quickly addressed. A new middle class had appeared, and optimism was widespread. While much of the area still appeared rural, Westminster's agricultural basis was rapidly disappearing.

In 1957, the city finally incorporated. Originally, it was intended to include Westminster, Barber City, and Midway City under the name Tri-Cities. But Midway City opted out, and the name was quickly changed to Westminster. The first city hall was in Sigler Park, and the newly formed city council made plans for several new grammar schools and junior high schools. Westminster's first high school opened in 1959. Progress was coming at a dizzying pace.

The city was developing fairly smoothly when, in 1961, the Eastgate bribery scandal occurred. It resulted in prison terms for the city manager and five city council members. The city had some difficulty recovering from this setback. Calvin Brack pointed out that Westminster received very little tax revenue from industry and was destined to be a housing community. He led a failed attempt to disincorporate in hopes of being annexed by Huntington Beach.

From 1960 to 1970, the now slightly more diverse population nearly doubled to 60,000, and the face of the city was completely changed. The landmark Green Kat was replaced by the stately Keystone Savings. After the old village center's decline, new locations for a possible downtown were being considered. The post office and library were moved to Goldenwest Shopping Center, where a Food Giant supermarket and a Bank of America were also built. A new civic center and courthouse appeared in early 1968. Opened in 1973, Westminster Mall became a critical source of tax revenue. The mall remained the commercial center of gravity of the city for the next two decades.

Similarly to the settlement's early period, Westminster's fraternal organizations played an important unifying role during the early years of rapid growth for the city. The sign in this photograph, located on Beach Boulevard just north of the Hiway 39 Drive-In, features the Lions and Optimist club shields as the first to be hung on the first city limits sign at that location.

During the months preceding the city's incorporation in 1957, the west side of Westminster was quickly establishing itself as a booming bedroom community. Housing tracts like Indian Village, whose newly graded roads are visible left of center in this photograph, preceded shopping centers, supermarkets, and schools. Johnson Junior High School, Finley Elementary School, and Westminster High School were yet to be built. Within 10 years, there would be four supermarkets on Westminster Boulevard between Goldenwest Street and Springdale Street.

Anticipating the future development of Orange County in 1955, First Western established the first bank in Westminster history. It resided at a storefront on Westminster Boulevard, near Pacific Street, for two years until a new 8,200-square-foot, one-story building was constructed on the nearby corner of Westminster Boulevard and Cardillo Street. It was designed by architect Robert Bennett of Pasadena and built at a cost of $350,000. Its first manager was James Allen. Two years later, First Western Bank would open a new branch in neighboring Stanton.

Before the onset of the housing boom of the 1960s, New Westminster had merged with the newly incorporated city. The auto parts store on the left still bore the name of the original development. The field on the south side across the street from it was the previous site of George Murdock's onion farm. It is the present site of the civic center, county courthouse, and library. The auto parts building is still standing today on property once belonging to the colony's first settler, John Anderson. (Courtesy Orange County Archives.)

Longtime resident George Meinhardt was a blacksmith elected to the city's first city council. He was the city's first mayor and during 1960 was swept up in the Eastgate bribery scandal. His conviction was set aside by presiding judge Ronald Crookshank because of questions about some of the testimony. After taking a lie detector test in 1962, charges against him were dropped. There is a street in Westminster named after him.

Jay C. Decker was a businessman elected to Westminster's first city council during the special election to incorporate Westminster in 1957. His wife was an elementary school principal. They arrived in the Orange County area in 1945. He served for a year before losing to Gene Allison in the general election in 1958. Decker was the only member of the first city council who was not involved in the Eastgate bribery scandal.

In 1994, cleanup efforts began at the Ralph Gray Superfund site in a housing tract (left of center in the photograph) on the east side of Goldenwest Boulevard, south of Hazard Avenue. Oil refinery waste had been dumped there during the mid-1930s, and globs of black toxic sludge were oozing to the surface in backyards. Accommodations in extended-stay hotels and rental houses were found for residents, who had to wait until August 1995 to return to their homes. They became known in the press as "toxic refugees." This Superfund site was considered unique in that the toxic waste was found in a residential area, where houses had been built on top of it.

Suburban housing tracts, soon to become ubiquitous, make an early appearance in this aerial view from 1958 looking north. In the lower right is the intersection of Bolsa Avenue and Goldenwest Boulevard, where the Pacific Goldfish Farm, owned by Henry Akiyama, was located on the corner. The future site of Westminster High School is above the tract of homes in the center of the photograph. At center on the far right side is the location of the Ralph Gray Trucking Company Superfund site.

Following the resignation of the city council because of the Eastgate bribery scandal, the new city council faced daunting challenges in the new city. The public's confidence in its city's government was at a low point as the council struggled to regain its credibility. Joseph Svogar served as mayor following George Meinhardt's resignation in August 1961. Liquor store owner Cal Brack took over as mayor in February 1962 when Svogar resigned and moved to San Francisco. After Brack's term ended, he began a campaign for the disincorporation of the city, contending that lack of tax revenue from businesses would lead Westminster toward increasingly dense housing.

Anaheim developers Doyle and Shields had already found success in Anaheim when they decided to build Westminster Square Shopping Center on the corner of Edwards Street and Westminster Boulevard in 1958. The developers also built the tract of homes behind the center. In 1960, Westminster Lanes opened and quickly became popular. The 32-lane bowling alley was built at a cost of $800,000 and was designed by architect Donald Barker. When it opened, it included a restaurant, cocktail lounge, and banquet room.

City council members Art Paysen (second from left) and Gordon Dorfsmith (second from right) joined store officials for the grand opening of Thrifty Drug Store in 1964. Along with Kress and Food Giant, the pharmacy served as an anchor store for the newly developed Goldenwest Shopping Center. At one point during this era, there were four supermarkets in the one-mile distance between Springdale Street and Goldenwest Street on Westminster Boulevard.

In 1958, Barney Edwards's bean ranch on Goldenwest Street was chosen as the site for Westminster's new high school. It was to be the second high school in the Huntington Beach Union High School District. Construction began on the school in June of that year. The school was intended to accommodate students from eight grammar schools in the Westminster School District.

Westminster High School opened in September 1959, although many of the buildings were still incomplete. Construction strikes and steel shortages delayed completion of the gym until January 1960. The library was finished a month later.

Charles Mashburn was named the first principal of Westminster High School in 1957. Mashburn, vice principal of Huntington Beach High School at the time, would not take the position until the school opened in 1959. Two years later, the school had 1,900 students. In 1962, Mashburn was promoted to a district-level position as director of services and recreation. He was followed by Ferren Christensen, who served in an interim position before being named principal in 1964.

The 1960 Founders Day celebration included a parade, beauty pageant, several dances, and a carnival. The parade included 24 jeeps, each carrying a candidate in the pageant. The theme of the festivities honoring the city's 84th birthday hearkened back to "Old Time Days," and there was a beard-growing contest.

Dr. Russell Johnson's years-long effort to build a hospital in Westminster culminated in the opening of Westminster Hospital in 1959. Located on Hospital Circle near Twenty-First Street and Arizona Street, the 20,000-square-foot building cost $700,000 and was owned by Powers Brothers of Los Angeles. It was acquired by Humana Incorporated in 1983, and its name was changed to Westminster Community Hospital. It was sold to Vencor in 1992 and became Kindred Hospital, a long-term acute care hospital.

Westminster Chapel opened with the new mortuary at Westminster Memorial Park in January 1960. They both were built at a cost of $300,000 and were designed by Long Beach architects Palmer Power and Delma Daniels. The distinctive A-frame Mid-Century Modern chapel has a 40-foot-high roof and stained-glass windows on both sides. Pews can accommodate 168 persons, and the family room can hold 40.

By the early 1960s, Westminster's professional fire department had formed from the earlier volunteer group. In 1960, a new building was constructed on Goldenwest Street, just south of Westminster Boulevard. It was 4,600 square feet and was built at a cost of $55,000. It served as headquarters of the fire department until a new one was built at Olive Street and Westminster Boulevard.

Following Westminster's first police chief Clint Wright's resignation in 1958, Conner Collacott (center) first assumed duties in August. Collacott had served as a police officer in Ventura for nine years and had advanced to lieutenant before moving to Westminster. He headed the police department during the city's population boom of the 1960s. He was fired in August 1966 over an indiscretion with a woman that had occurred some years previously. The support for Collacott included a group of women who joined together to effectively protest the firing. The backlash caused the city council to change its mind, and he was reinstated early the next year. He retired in 1971 and went on to serve on the city council in 1978. He was also a board member of the Midway City Sanitation District. Collacott died in January 1982.

During the height of tiki culture's popularity, Gray's Nursery on Beach Boulevard featured the work of famed tiki and mask carver Milan Guanko, originally from the Philippines. His workshop was in Anaheim near Disneyland. During construction of the park, Disney bought some of his work and supplied him with recently cut down palm trees. Guanko's artistic influence was pervasive. His tikis were in hotels and resorts around the world and are still prized today. The Kon Tiki Bar in Tucson has a large collection of his work.

The 1967 Founders Day parade was the largest to date with 186 entries. Miss Westminster Shelley Bozarth graced the city's float, celebrating its 10th anniversary. Garden Grove won the sweepstakes prize with a colorful float. It touted its city's Strawberry Festival and featured five pretty girls in the place of strawberries. Warner and Stacey intermediate school bands won in the junior band division.

Sequoia School, on Iroquois Street west of Springdale Street, is located in the middle of a tract of homes that were built nearly at the same time as the school in 1963. This artist's rendering of the school accurately depicts the layout of the buildings as they were constructed. Adams, Morgan, Lathem, Kripp, and Wright were a well-regarded architectural and engineering firm in Long Beach. Some of the streets in the tract around the school were named after Westminster's first city council members.

The landmark Green Kat Café, built around 1930, was on the southwest corner of Beach Boulevard and Westminster Boulevard. It was originally called the Green Gables and was an early example of the Tudor Revival style of architecture that would later become a Westminster signature. It had a reputation as being mildly notorious and was said to be at one time the only traffic signal between Knott's Berry Farm and the beach. It closed in 1962, was torn down, and was replaced by future Orange County supervisor Ron Caspers's Keystone Savings and Loan.

Around 1960, the Hoover School was closed and repurposed for use as the city hall and council chambers. The police department was moved there as well. From the city's incorporation in 1957 until the relocation, a small building in Sigler Park had housed a city office and room for council meetings.

Mel Ingram was the first fire chief for the newly formed volunteer fire department in Westminster in 1950. He later became the fire chief when the city first formed. He was the building director for newly incorporated Westminster during the late 1950s, overseeing the first wave of the population boom the area was beginning to experience. During the 1960s, Ingram was president of the Orange County Fire Chiefs Association.

The serpentine lines on Bolsa Avenue were designed to alert drivers in the fog to an oncoming intersection, in this case Brookhurst Boulevard. This is the site of the early Sears Settlement from the 1870s, later to be called Bolsa. By 1963, the year this photograph was taken looking west, Westminster could still be subject to very intense fog attracted to moist areas. As more of the farmlands were replaced with housing tracts and commercial developments, the fog diminished until the early 21st century, when it almost entirely disappeared. (Courtesy Orange County Archives.)

In early 1966, Keystone Savings Bank owner Ron Caspers opened the Ha' Penny Inn next to his bank, located at Beach Boulevard and Westminster Boulevard. It was the most sumptuous and elegant restaurant Westminster had seen. Built at a cost of $1 million, the architecture followed the Tudor Revival theme of the bank. It evoked 18th-century English inns with clay shingles, hand-hewn double doors, and a cobblestone drive lit by gas lanterns. The interior included half-timbered used brick walls, antique furniture, and a bar featuring an array of embedded halfpennies. After Caspers's death in 1977, it became the Bell and Crown before becoming Victoria Station. It was called Westminster Manor when it was demolished to make way for a Starbucks in 2017.

In 1961, Ron Caspers acquired the legendary Green Kat, and by 1963, he had replaced one Westminster landmark with another. After buying out Westminster Savings and Loan, he built Keystone Bank on the southwest corner of Beach Boulevard and Westminster Boulevard. It became the iconic half-timbered brick representation of Westminster's Tudor Revival–style architecture. A feature, including seven photographs, was published in *Architectural Digest* in the fall of its opening year. Keystone Savings and Loan Association, of which Caspers was president, boasted resources of $25 million. During the grand opening, the bank displayed a million dollars cash in the lobby of the bank. (Courtesy Huntington Library, San Marino, California.)

Honorary Westminster historian Edna Richards's work on the city's colony and pioneer period formed the basis for the Westminster Historical Museum. She located and interviewed descendants of the early settlers, collecting photographs, material, and interviews for her unpublished "Westminster Profiles." Richards and her husband, Tom, were avid gardeners, and she headed the Beautification Committee for the unincorporated city during the 1950s. Born in Oklahoma in 1902, she passed away in 1988.

Construction of a new library in the shopping center at Goldenwest Street and Westminster Boulevard began in October 1962. Seven months later, county supervisor C.M. Featherly was the master of ceremonies at its dedication. The new building was six times larger than its predecessor at Sigler Park, and the collection more than doubled its size. Orange County Public Library signed a 10-year lease at $645 a month. When the lease ended, arrangements were made to accommodate the library until it moved to the new civic center in 1977.

Westminster Center, on the northwest corner of Goldenwest Street and Westminster Boulevard, was built in 1959. The property was owned by the Nakawatase family. The center was designed by the Barondon Corporation of Los Angeles, and the 40 acres were developed at a cost of $4 million. By 1959, it included the post office, a Food Giant supermarket, Thrifty Drug Store, Bank of America, and the Kress Store. The center was successful through the 1960s and into the early 1970s. (Courtesy Orange County Archives.)

In 1974, Orange County Public Library officials accepted the site behind the civic center as a suitable location for the new library building. The site had initially been rejected by them for being too hidden from view. Librarian Lionel Ascher and the expanded collection moved from the old location to the new 18,000-square-foot redbrick building designed by William Blurock and Partners during the fall of 1977. The library continues to serve the community from this location.

In September 1998, one of Westminster's two reservoirs suffered a rupture in its side that was 25 feet high and 22 feet long. The resultant five-million-gallon flood rushed into a neighboring townhouse complex on Hefley Street, injuring a responding firefighter and three civilians. Fifty structures were damaged, and 150 residents had to be evacuated. Previous inspections and later investigations cited a number of issues with the 30-year-old reservoir, which had not been maintained properly. Two new reservoirs were built at the corner of Hoover Street and Hazard Avenue near a drainage channel between it and a nearby residential area.

In 1968, Derek McWhinney and Joy Neugebauer were the newest members of the city council when it elected them mayor and vice mayor. McWhinney would remain mayor until 1973, when he resigned during a bribery scandal. In 1984, Neugebauer would become both Westminster's first popularly elected and woman mayor. Council member Phil Anthony would later become an Orange County supervisor.

Edwards Cinema West opened on August 5, 1966, at the Westminster Shopping Center near the library. It featured the twin bill of *Around the World Under the Sea* and the James Bond film *Thunderball*. It had 900 seats and was the 36th theater in the Edwards Theater chain and its third Orange County location. It added a twin theater in July 1970. The theater was demolished in 1991 as part of the remodeling of the shopping center and reopened a year later nearby as Edwards Westminster 10.

In 1966, Westminster High School's cheerleading squad consisted of, from left to right, Alice Green, Chris Anderson, Michele Solomon, Tom Landers, and Sue Dougherty. They are seen here leading the cheering at the pre-game rally for the homecoming game. That year, there were 3,000 students in the student body with 640 graduating seniors. Westminster Lions football star Rikki Aldridge played later in the year for the South in the annual North/South Shrine Classic.

Phil Anthony was first elected to Westminster's city council in 1962 and served as mayor from 1972 until 1976. He was elected and served on the county board of supervisors from 1976 to 1981, chairing the board in 1979. After a minor setback regarding campaign donations, he began serving on the board of the Orange County Water District. There, he pioneered important water replenishment systems, for which he won awards from the Groundwater Foundation and the California Sierra Club in 2018. During his last years, he was vigorously opposed to the Poseidon desalination project in Huntington Beach.

Construction began on the new $4.3-million civic center on Westminster Boulevard near Beach Boulevard in August 1967. The first phase of building on the 20-acre site included the library, council chambers, a police building, and a clock tower. For a short time, the library was used as an administration building and for community services, while the police building housed some administration offices. The civic center was dedicated in June 1968. It was designed to serve a population of 100,000 people. The population of Westminster was 53,000 at this time.

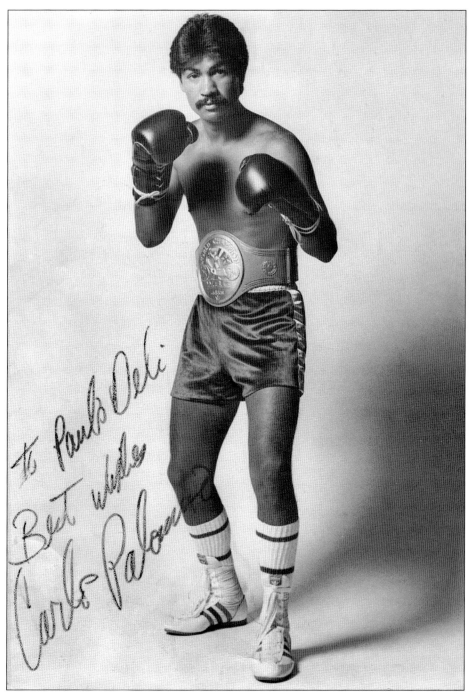

To Paulo Deli
Best wishes
Carlos Palomino

Former world welterweight boxing champion Carlos Palomino was born in Mexico and raised in Santa Ana and Westminster. After graduating from Westminster High School, he served in the Army in 1971 and 1972. He won the World Boxing Council crown in 1976 with a stunning upset over champion John Stracey in London and held the championship until 1979. Following his boxing career, he found some success as a spokesman for Miller Lite Beer. He was inducted into the International Boxing Hall of Fame in 2004. (Courtesy Junior at Paul's Deli, Westminster, California.)

The concrete wall of the handball court at Sigler Park was used for tagging and graffiti until the city contracted Santa Ana artist Gil Vasquez to paint a mural on it. *The Assumption of the Virgin Mary* was one of the very few examples of public art in Westminster until the arrival of the Vietnamese immigrants in 1977. He worked on the mural for two months before completing it in June 1978.

Fr. Joseph Murrin was pastor at Blessed Sacrament Church from 1967 until 1973. During this period, he hosted a visit to the school by Gov. Ronald Reagan. Father Murrin had been an assistant to Fr. John McFadden during the parish's early formation from 1945 to 1947. In 1967, he oversaw the remodelling of the rectory reception room and offices. He was pastor when the Presbyterian Social Hall (or "Small Hall" to parishioners) was demolished in 1971.

Members of the community assisted Vasquez and learned techniques for painting a mural. Vasquez went on to create two other murals in Santa Ana and one at California State University, Fullerton. His mural in Westminster is the last one still in existence. He still creates art in a variety of media in Santa Ana.

Construction began on Westminster Mall at Goldenwest Street and Bolsa Avenue in September 1972. It was built by Homart Developers, a subsidiary of Sears, Roebuck and Company. The project cost approximately $50 million, $6 million of which was invested by Sears. The 92-acre site with 6,200 parking spaces and 176 stores was one of the largest in Southern California at the time. Anchor stores included Sears, May Company, Buffum's, and Robinson's. The new mall proved to be a boon to the local economy, supplying hundreds of jobs and tax revenue for the city.

In January 1977, Westminster's first mayor, George Meinhardt (far right), met with the city's first woman mayor, Joy Neugebauer (second from right), at Westminster Mall. Originally from Illinois, Neugebauer and her husband and family moved to Westminster in the mid-1950s. They founded Ace Tools in Long Beach. Widowed in 1975, she continued to operate the business for 19 years while raising a family and pursuing her career in politics. Neugebauer was important in the founding of the Leaora Blakey Historical Park. She would later serve as president of the Westminster Historical Society until she passed away in 2022.

The McCoy-Hare House was moved next to the chamber of commerce on Hazard Avenue near Beach Boulevard, restored, and dedicated in August 1977. Janet Reynolds was the program chairperson for the dedication. The home was originally next door to Hare's Garage on Westminster Boulevard. The higher-peaked building, constructed by Dr. McCoy in 1873, was the second pharmacy in Westminster. Orel and Marie Hare purchased it in 1912 and added rooms over the decades. Their son, motorcycle speed record holder Bud Hare, grew up and later lived in this house.

Six

LITTLE SAIGON
AND A NEW ERA
1977–PRESENT DAY

The first Vietnamese refugees arrived in Westminster after the end of the Vietnam War in 1975. They settled near Bolsa Avenue between Brookhurst Avenue and Magnolia Avenue, an area which had been in commercial decline for some years. Many of the early arrivals were from cities, were educated, and spoke English. Several factors, including climate, social services, and inexpensive real estate, made the area an attractive location for this new ethnic enclave.

The new settlers faced a variety of challenges. The language and cultural barriers were formidable. While many residents were sympathetic to the plight of the refugees, there was backlash from some against the new immigrants. But as word of Little Saigon spread, it began to draw people from across the country.

Commercial development came fairly quickly. Soon small businesses appeared in storefronts and small shopping centers. Danh's Pharmacy, one of the first Vietnamese-owned businesses, opened in 1978. Little Saigon's oldest and largest newspaper, *Nguoi Viet News*, was established the same year. Developer Frank Jao bought property and laid out the business sector along Bolsa Avenue. Jao's original vision of an "Asiantown" resulted in Asian Garden Village and the landmark Asian Garden Mall. But his proposed bridge over Bolsa Avenue met with the criticism that it diluted the community's identity and was rejected.

Continued progress resulted in local political advances. In 1992, city council member Tony Lam became the first Vietnamese-born elected official in this country, and more would follow. The Hi-Tek demonstrations in 2000 further solidified the role of anti-Communism as a central socially unifying force in the community. In 1999, Tri Ta became the first elected mayor in the United States born in Vietnam.

Little Saigon's growth and prosperity continues to the present day. Westminster, Garden Grove, and Santa Ana have become home to the largest concentration of Vietnamese people outside of Vietnam. Bolsa, as the section of Little Saigon in Westminster is known, is widely viewed as the "capital" of the Vietnamese diaspora in the United States. This vibrant community has redefined Westminster and created a new identity for the city.

Refugees from the Vietnam War first started arriving at Marine Corps Base Camp Pendelton in Oceanside, California, with the fall of Saigon in late April 1975. Camp Pendelton was one of four destinations in the United States chosen for the relocation of 130,000 Vietnamese refugees from several different staging islands in the Pacific Ocean. A total of 260 refugees, more than half of them children, arrived by bus from Norton Air Force Base near San Bernardino as part of Operation New Arrivals. Within 45 days, civilian agencies would resettle them in various locations. (Courtesy Orange County Archives.)

Westminster Night at Angel Stadium was held on May 2, 1979. In attendance were, from left to right, Mayor Bill French, chamber of commerce president Bob Lewis, Angel player Bobby Grich, Miss Westminster Valerie Powell, and city council member Elden Gillespie. Widely respected by the Vietnamese community, Gillespie became a pivotal figure as mayor on the council while Little Saigon began to develop its political power. After Gillespie died, Vietnamese council member Tony Lam said, "We consider him our godfather." Gillespie was 71 years old when he passed away in 1988.

Pharmacist Dr. Quach Danh fled North Vietnam when the war ended and was among the first Vietnamese refugees to arrive in the United States. He was fluent in English, went to pharmacy school in Nebraska, and attained a license. He and his family then settled in Westminster, where he opened a pharmacy in 1978. It was one of the first Vietnamese-owned businesses to be established on Bolsa Avenue. Not long after this, his wife opened a second pharmacy. Danh's pharmacy served an important role in assisting the growing new community by providing medical assistance to new non-English speaking refugees.

RE-ELECT
WESTMINSTER COUNCILMAN

TONY LAM

COMMUNITY BUILDER
TAX FIGHTER
CRIME FIGHTER

VOTE NOVEMBER 3, 1998

In 1992, self-described "three-time refugee" Tony Lam became the first Vietnamese-born US citizen to be elected to public office in this country. His main support in this election came from non-Vietnamese voters. Lam's family fled North Vietnam in 1954 after the defeat of the French by resistance forces at Dien Bien Phu. From 1963 to 1975, he worked in various capacities with the US government until he and his family had to flee from Saigon. He became camp manager at the refugee camp in Guam, serving 125,000 people. After coming to Little Saigon, he organized the first Tet festival in 1981. He met severe criticism in the Vietnamese community for his silence during the Hi-Tek incident in 1999. After serving three terms, he decided not to run again in 2002.

As an indication of the evolving status of the community, Little Saigon was designated by the city as a tourist zone and a redevelopment project in February 1988. A few months later, Gov. George Deukmejian displayed new freeway directional signs at Asian Garden Mall that were soon to be installed. Tony Lam lobbied for this and was supported by the city council and the city's redevelopment agency. (Courtesy Grant Hartwell.)

Built in 1987 and located on Bolsa Avenue in the heart of Little Saigon, the landmark Asian Garden Mall (or Phuoc Loc Tho in Vietnamese) is the largest Vietnamese shopping center in the United States. Its name reflected developer Frank Jao's original vision of Little Saigon as "Asiantown," an idea that eventually gave way to a more Vietnamese-centered view of the community. The mall has become a tourist destination for Vietnamese across the United States and is a source of pride for the immigrant community. (Courtesy Orange County Archives.)

Westminster's first three women mayors, (left to right) Joy Neugebauer, Margie Rice, and Kathy Buchoz, pose for a photograph taken by Mayor Tri Ta. The three were pivotal figures during the establishment of the Little Saigon community and a period of transition of political power in Westminster. Buchoz worked closely with developer Frank Jao during the early stages of the development of the new Vietnamese community. (Courtesy Kathy Buchoz.)

The publishers of the Rosemead-based *Saigon Times*, Cam Ai Tran and Hap Tu, led a 10-year effort to build the Vietnamese Boat People Memorial. In 2009, the memorial was dedicated at Westminster Memorial Park. Located in the park's southeast corner, it consists of a sculpture and fountain surrounded by 54 stone blocks inscribed with the names of 6,000 refugees who died trying to flee Vietnam by boat after 1975.

The California Zoroastrian Center building, called Rustam Guiv Dar-e Mehr, is located on Hazard Street near Newland Street. It cost $536,000 to build and was 8,000 square feet when it opened in March 1987. A two-story annex was added the next year. The center serves religious functions and social needs for the Southern California Persian community. The building contains a fire altar, originally from India, that is over 100 years old.

Many Westminster residents were unaware of the historic Mendez anti-segregation decision when the US Postal Service issued a 41¢ commemorative stamp celebrating its 60th anniversary on September 17, 2007. The stamp was illustrated by Mexico City artist Raphael Lopez, who had a studio in San Diego. Sylvia Mendez would later be awarded the Presidential Medal of Freedom in 2011. (Courtesy Jim Tortolano.)

The Vietnam War Memorial in Sid Goldstein Freedom Park held unveiling ceremonies in April 2003. An estimated crowd of 9,000 people attended the dedication of the memorial. Frank Fry initiated the $1.2-million project while serving as mayor in 1996. The statue by sculptor Tuan Nguyen of two soldiers, one American and one Vietnamese, paid tribute to the soldiers of both countries who died during the Vietnam War. It was noted at the time that this was one of the few occasions that the flag of South Vietnam was publicly flown.

Nguoi Viet Daily News was founded and first published out of a garage in San Diego in 1978 by Yen Ngoc Do and his wife, Loan La Do. Now based in Westminster, it is the oldest, largest, and most influential Vietnamese newspaper in the United States. Viewed today as the founder of Vietnamese-language media in this country, Do passed away in 2006. Their eldest daughter, Anh Do, is a journalist and covers Little Saigon for the *Los Angeles Times*. (Courtesy Grant Hartwell.)

The annual Tet celebrations of the Lunar New Year have been held in Little Saigon, sometimes separately in Westminster and neighboring Garden Grove, since the early 1980s. It soon became the largest Vietnamese observance of the new year in the country. A parade became popular, and the event began to draw tens of thousands of people. Floats, dragons, marching bands, food, and pink and yellow blossoms grace Bolsa Avenue during this community's much anticipated event. (Courtesy Jim Tortolano.)

The soup dish *pho* originated in Vietnam in the early 20th century and entered the mainstream in the United States during the 1990s. Owners Tho Tran and Lieu Tran opened Pho 79 on Hazard Avenue in 1982. In 2019, their restaurant was recognized by James Beard and included in his prestigious America's Classics.

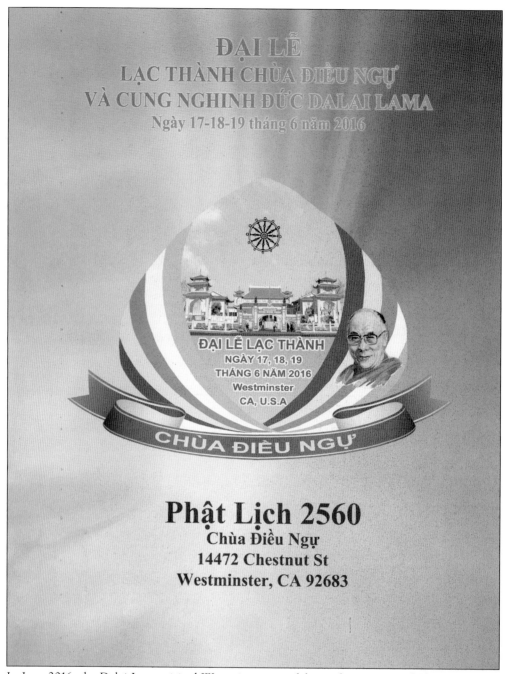

In June 2016, the Dalai Lama visited Westminster to celebrate the opening of Chua Dieu Ngu Buddhist temple on Chestnut Street. The widely respected spiritual leader is an icon throughout the world and in the Vietnamese community. An estimated 6,000 people came to hear the Dalai Lama speak of kindness and compassion.

In 2012, Tri Ta (left, with the Dalai Lama) became the first elected Vietnamese-born mayor in the United States. He was reelected mayor twice in the following four years. He was born in Saigon in 1973 and moved to this country with his family when he was 19. He earned a bachelor of arts in political science in 1998 and worked as a career consultant and employment counselor. In 2022, Tri Ta was elected to California's state assembly. (Courtesy Jim Tortolano.)

Buddhism is the most widely practiced religion in Little Saigon. The Chua Dieu Ngu Buddhist temple originally opened in a warehouse on Chestnut Street, near Hazard Avenue, in 2008. A large new structure was built adjacent to it and opened in March 2016. The 20,000-square-foot structure, featuring distinctive traditional architecture, was built at a cost of $6 million. The following year, the Dalai Lama visited Westminster at the invitation of Thich Vien Ly, the abbott of the temple.

DISCOVER THOUSANDS OF LOCAL HISTORY BOOKS FEATURING MILLIONS OF VINTAGE IMAGES

Arcadia Publishing, the leading local history publisher in the United States, is committed to making history accessible and meaningful through publishing books that celebrate and preserve the heritage of America's people and places.

Find more books like this at
www.arcadiapublishing.com

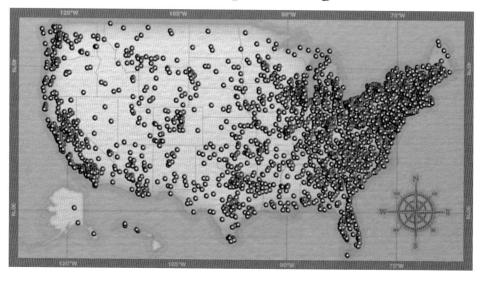

Search for your hometown history, your old stomping grounds, and even your favorite sports team.

Consistent with our mission to preserve history on a local level, this book was printed in South Carolina on American-made paper and manufactured entirely in the United States. Products carrying the accredited Forest Stewardship Council (FSC) label are printed on 100 percent FSC-certified paper.

MADE IN THE